History of the Incas
BY
Pedro Sarmiento de Gamboa

INTRODUCTION.

The publication of the text of the Sarmiento manuscript in the Library of Göttingen University, has enabled the Council to present the members of the Hakluyt Society with the most authentic narrative of events connected with the history of the Incas of Peru.

The history of this manuscript, and of the documents which accompanied it, is very interesting. The Viceroy, Don Francisco de Toledo, who governed Peru from 1569 to 1581, caused them to be prepared for the information of Philip II. Four cloths were sent to the King from Cuzco, and a history of the Incas written by Captain Pedro Sarmiento de Gamboa. On three cloths were figures of the Incas with their wives, on medallions, with their Ayllus and a genealogical tree. Historical events in each reign were depicted on the borders. The fable of Tampu-tocco was shown on the first cloth, and also the fables touching the creations of Viracocha, which formed the foundation for the whole history. On the fourth cloth there was a map of Peru, the compass lines for the positions of towns being drawn by Sarmiento.

The Viceroy also caused reports to be made to him, to prove that the Incas were usurpers. There were thirteen reports from Cuzco, Guamanga, Xauxa, Yucay, and other places, forming a folio of 213 leaves, preserved in the Archivo de Indias[1]. At Cuzco all the Inca descendants were called upon to give evidence respecting the history of Peru under their ancestors. They all swore that they would give truthful testimony. The compilation of the history was then entrusted to Captain Pedro Sarmiento de Gamboa, the cosmographer of Peru. When it was completed the book was read to the Inca witnesses, chapter by chapter, in their own language. They discussed each chapter, and suggested some corrections and alterations which were adopted. It was then submitted to the Viceroy, who caused the documents to be attested by the principal Spaniards settled at Cuzco, who had been present at the conquest, or had taken a leading part in the subsequent administration. These were Dr Loarte, the licentiate Polo de Ondegardo[2], Alonso de Mena[3], Mancio Serra de Leguisano[4], Pero Alonso Carrasco, and Juan de Pancorvo[5], in whose house the Viceroy resided while he was at Cuzco. Mancio Serra de Leguisano married Beatriz Ñusta, an Inca princess, daughter of Huayna Ccapac. The Viceroy then made some final interpolations to vilify the Incas, which would not have been approved by some of those who had attested, certainly not by Polo de Ondegardo or Leguisano.

[Note 1: Printed in the same volume with Montesinos, and edited by Jimenes de la Espada, Informaciones acerca del señorio y gobierno de los Ingas hechas por mandado de Don Francisco de Toledo, 1570—72.]

[Note 2: The accomplished lawyer, author, and statesman.]

[Note 3: One of the first conquerors. His house at Cuzco was in the square of our Lady, near that of Garcilasso de la Vega.]

[Note 4: A generous defender of the cause of the Indians.]

[Note 5: One of the first conquerors. He occupied a house near the square, with his friend and comrade Alonso de Marchena.]

Sarmiento mentions in his history of the Incas that it was intended to be the Second Part of his work. There were to be three Parts. The First, on the geography of Peru, was not sent because it was not finished. The Third Part was to have been a narrative of the conquest.

The four cloths, and the other documents, were taken to Spain, for presentation to the King, by a servant of the Viceroy named Geronimo Pacheco, with a covering letter dated at Yucay on March 1st, 1572.

Of all these precious documents the most important was the history of the Incas by Sarmiento, and it has fortunately been preserved. The King's copy found its way into the famous library of Abraham Gronovius, which was sold in 1785, and thence into the library of the University of Göttingen, where it remained, unprinted and unedited, for 120 years. But in August, 1906, the learned librarian, Dr Richard Pietschmann published the text at Berlin, very carefully edited and annotated with a valuable introduction. The Council of the Hakluyt Society is thus enabled to present an English translation to its members very soon after the first publication of the text. It is a complement of the other writings of the great navigator, which were translated and edited for the Hakluyt Society in 1895.

The manuscript consists of eight leaves of introduction and 138 of text. The dedicatory letter to the King is signed by Sarmiento on March 4th, 1572. The binding was of red silk, under which there is another binding of green leather. The first page is occupied by a coloured shield of the royal arms, with a signature el Capitã Sarmi de Gãboa. On the second page is the title, surrounded by an ornamental border. The manuscript is in a very clear hand, and at the end are the arms of Toledo (chequy azure and argent) with the date Cuzco, 29 Feb., 1572. There is also the signature of the Secretary, Alvaro Ruiz de Navamuel[6].

[Note 6: Alvaro Ruiz and his brother Captain Francisco Ruiz were the sons of Francisco Santiago Rodriguez de los Rios by Inez de Navamuel. Both used their mother's name of Navamuel as their surname; and both were born at Aquilar del Campo. Alonso Ruiz de Navamuel was Secretary to the governments of five successive Viceroys. He wrote a Relacion de las cosas mas notables que hiza en el Peru, siendo Virev Don Francisco de Toledo, 20 Dec. 1578. He died in the year 1613. The descendants of his son Juan de los Rios formed the mayorazgos of Rios and Cavallero.

By his wife Angela Ortiz de Arbildo y Berriz, a Biscayan, he had a daughter Inez married to her cousin Geronimo Aliaga, a son of the Secretary's brother Captain Francisco Ruiz de Navamuel, the encomendero of Caracoto in the Collao, by Juana, daughter of Captain Geronimo de Aliaga. His marriage, at which the Viceroy Toledo was present, took place on November 23rd, 1578. From the marriage of the younger Geronimo de Aliaga with Inez Navamuel, descend the Aliagas, Counts of Luringancho in Peru.]

The history of the Incas by Sarmiento is, without any doubt, the most authentic and reliable that has yet appeared. For it was compiled from the carefully attested evidence of the Incas themselves, taken under official sanction. Each sovereign Inca formed an ayllu or "gens" of his descendants, who preserved the memory of his deeds in quipus, songs, and traditions handed down and learnt by heart. There were many descendants of each of these ayllus living near Cuzco in 1572, and the leading members were examined on oath; so that Sarmiento had opportunities of obtaining accurate information which no other writer possessed. For the correct versions of the early traditions, and for historical facts and the chronological order of events, Sarmiento is the best authority.

But no one can supersede the honest and impartial old soldier, Pedro de Cieza de Leon, as regards the charm of his style and the confidence to be placed in his opinions; nor the Inca Garcilasso de la Vega as regards his reminiscences and his fascinating love for his people. Molina and Yamqui Pachacuti give much fuller details respecting the ceremonial festivals and religious beliefs. Polo de Ondegardo and Santillana supply much fuller and more reliable information respecting the laws and administration of the Incas. It is in the historical narrative and the correct order of events that Sarmiento, owing to his exceptional means of collecting accurate information, excels all other writers.

There is one serious blemish. Sarmiento's book was written, not only or mainly to supply interesting information, but with an object. Bishop Las Casas had made Europe ring with the cruelties of the Spaniards in the Indies, and with the injustice and iniquity of their conquests. Don Francisco de Toledo used this narrative for the purpose of making a feeble reply to the good bishop. Under his instructions Sarmiento stated the Viceroy's argument, which was that the King of Spain was the rightful sovereign of Peru because the Incas had usurped their power by conquest and had been guilty of acts of cruelty. Hence the constant repetition of such phrases as "cruel tyranny" and "usurping tyrant"; and the numerous interpolations of the Viceroy himself are so obvious that I have put them in italics within brackets. He goes back as far as the first Inca to make out the usurpation, and he is always harping on illegitimacy. If we go back as far as Sancho IV the title of Philip II to Spain was voided by the grossest usurpation, while we need only go back to Henry II to see how Philip's title was vitiated by illegitimacy. As for cruelty, it would be a strange plea from the sovereign by whose orders the Netherlands were devastated, the Moors of Granada almost annihilated, and under whose rule the Inquisition was in full swing. It is the old story of preaching without practice, as Dr Newman once observed in quoting what James I said to George Heriot:

"O Geordie, jingling Geordie, it was grand to hear Baby Charles laying down the guilt of dissimulation, and Steenie lecturing on the turpitude of incontinence."

It is right to say that Philip never seems to have endorsed the argument of his Viceroy, while his father prohibited the circulation of a book by Dr Sepulveda which contained a similar argument; nor was the work of Sarmiento published.

Barring this blemish, the history of the Incas, written by order of the Viceroy Toledo, is a most valuable addition to the authorities who have given us authentic accounts of Andean civilization; for we may have every confidence in the care and accuracy of Sarmiento as regards his collection and statement of historical facts, provided that we always keep in mind the bias, and the orders he was under, to seek support for the Viceroy's untenable argument.

I have given all I have been able to find respecting the life of Sarmiento in the introduction to my edition of the voyages of that celebrated navigator.

But the administration of the Viceroy Don Francisco de Toledo, from 1569 to 1581, forms a landmark in the history of Peru, and seems to call for some notice in this place. He found the country in an unsettled state, with the administrative system entirely out of gear. Though no longer young he entered upon the gigantic task of establishing an orderly government, and resolved to visit personally every part of the vast territory under his rule. This stupendous undertaking occupied him for five years. He was accompanied by ecclesiastics, by men well versed in the language of the Incas and in their administrative policy, and by his secretary and aide-de-camp. These were the Bishop of Popayan, Augustin de la Coruña, the Augustine friars Juan Vivero and Francisco del Corral, the Jesuit and well-known author, Joseph de Acosta, the Inquisitor Pedro Ordoñez Flores, his brother, the Viceroy's chaplain and confessor, the learned lawyer Juan Matienzo, whose work is frequently quoted by Solorzano[7], the licentiate Polo de Ondegardo, who had been some years in the country and had acquired an intimate knowledge of the laws of the Incas, the secretary Alvaro Ruiz de Navamuel, and as aide-de-camp his young nephew, Geronimo de Figueroa, son of his brother Juan, the Ambassador at Rome[8].

[Note 7: In his Politica Indiana. There are two manuscripts of Juan Matienzo de Peralta at the British Museum, Govierno del Peru and Relacion del libro intitulado Govierno del Peru, apparently one work in two parts. Add. MSS. 5469, in Gayangos Catalogue, vol. II. p. 470.]

[Note 8: Some sons took the father's surname, others that of the mother. The Viceroy had the name of his father, Francisco Alvarez de Toledo, the third Count of Oropesa, while his brother Juan had the surname of Figueroa, being that of his mother.]

Toledo was endowed with indefatigable zeal for the public service, great energy, and extraordinary powers of application. He took the opinions of others, weighed them carefully, and considered long before he adopted any course. But he was narrow-minded and obstinate, and when he had once determined on a measure nothing could alter him. His ability is undoubted, and his appointment, at this particular juncture, is a proof of Philip's sagacity.

The Viceroy's intercourse with Polo de Ondegardo informed him respecting the administrative system of the Incas, so admirably adapted to the genius of the people, and he had the wisdom to see that there was much to learn from it. His policy was to collect the people, who, to a great extent, were scattered over the country and hiding from the Spaniards, in villages placed near the centres of their cultivated or pasture lands. He fixed the numbers in each village at 400 to 500, with a priest and Alcalde. He also ordered the boundaries of all the parishes to be settled. Spanish Corregidors were to take the places of the Tucuyricoc or governors of Inca times, and each village had an elected Alcalde approved by the Corregidor. Under him there were to be two overseers, a Pichca pachaca over 500, and a Pachaca as assistant. Another important measure was the settlement of the tribute. The name "tribute" was unfortunate. The system was that of the Incas, and the same which prevailed throughout the east. The government was the landlord, and the so-called "tribute" was rent. The Incas took two-thirds for the state and for religion, and set apart one-third for the cultivators. Toledo did much the same, assessing, according to the nature of the soil, the crops, and other local circumstances. For the formation of villages and the assessment of the tribute he promulgated a whole code of ordinances, many of them intended to prevent local oppression in various forms.

The Viceroy next took up the questions of the position of yana-cunas or domestic servants, and of forced service. Both these institutions existed in Incarial times. All that was needed were moderate laws for the protection of servants and conscripts, and the enforcement of such laws. Toledo allowed a seventh of the adult male population in each village to be made liable for service in mines or factories, fixed the distance they could be taken from their homes, and made rules for their proper treatment. It is true that the mita, as it was called, was afterwards an instrument of cruel oppression, that rules were disregarded, and that it depopulated the country. But this was not the fault of Toledo.

The Viceroy gave much attention to the mining industry, promoted the introduction of the use of mercury in the extraction of silver, and founded the town of Huancavelica near the quick-silver mine. His personality pervaded every department of the state, and his tasas or ordinances fill a large volume. He was a prolific legislator and a great statesman.

His worst mistake was the policy he adopted with regard to the family of the Incas. He desired to establish the position of the King of Spain without a rival. He, therefore, sought to malign the preceding dynasty, persecuted the descendants of the Incas, and committed one act of cruel injustice.

When Atahualpa put his half-brother Huascar, the last reigning Inca, to death, there remained three surviving sons of their father the great Inca Huayna Ccapac, named Manco, Paullu, and Titu Atauchi, and several daughters. After his occupation of Cuzco, Pizarro acknowledged Manco Inca as the legitimate successor of his brother Huascar, and he was publicly crowned, receiving all the insignia on March 24th, 1534. He escaped from the Spaniards and besieged them in Cuzco at the head of a large army. Forced to raise the siege he established his head-quarters at Ollantay-tampu, where he repulsed an attack led by Hernando Pizarro. He was, however, defeated by Orgoñiez, the lieutenant of Almagro, and took refuge in the mountainous province of Vilcapampa on the left bank of the Vilcamayu. From thence he made constant attacks on the Spaniards, maintaining his independence in this small remnant of his dominions. Some of the partisans of Almagro took refuge with him, and he was accidentally killed by one of them in 1544, after a not inglorious reign of ten years.

He left two legitimate sons, named Sayri Tupac and Tupac Amaru, by his wife and niece the Princess Ataria Cusi Huarcay, daughter of his ill-fated brother Huascar. This marriage was legalized by a bull of Pope Paul III in the time of the Viceroy Marquis of Cañete, 1555—1561. He had also an illegitimate son named Cusi Titu Yupanqui, and a daughter named Maria Tupac Usca, married to Don Pedro Ortiz de Orue, one of the first conquerors[9].

[Note 9: Diego Ortiz de Orue was born in the village of Getafe, near Madrid. He went out to Peru in 1559, and at once began to study the Quichua language. He was encomendero of Maras, a village overlooking the valley of Yucay. By the Inca princess he had a daughter named Catalina married to Don Luis Justiniani of Seville, descended from the Genoese family. Their son Luis was the grandfather of Dr Justo Pastor Justiniani who married Manuela Cataño, descended from Tupac Inca Yupanqui. Their son Don Pablo Justiniani was Cura of Laris until his death in 1858, and was a great depository of Inca lore. He had a very early copy of the Inca drama of Ollanta.]

Sayri Tupac succeeded as fourteenth Inca of Peru. On the arrival of the Marquis of Cañete as Viceroy in 1555, he caused overtures to be made to Sayri Tupac through his aunts, who were living at Cuzco with their Spanish husbands, Juan Sierra de Leguisano and Diego Hernandez. It was finally arranged that the Inca should receive 17000 castellanos of rent and the valley of Yucay. On October 7th, 1557, Sayri Tupac left Vilcapampa with 300 followers, reaching Andahuaylas on November 5th. He entered Lima on January 6th, 1558, was cordially greeted by the Viceroy and received investiture, assuming the names of Manco Ccapac Pachacuti Yupanqui. He went to live in the lovely vale of Yucay. He had been baptized with the name of Diego, but he did not long survive, dying at Yucay in 1560. His daughter Clara Beatriz married Don Martin Garcia Loyola. Their daughter Lorenza was created Marchioness of Oropesa and Yucay, with remainder to descendants of her great uncle Tupac Amaru. She was the wife of Juan Henriquez de Borja, grandson of the Duke of Gandia.

On the death of Sayri Tupac, his illegitimate brother, Cusi Titu Yupanqui assumed sovereignty, owing to the youth of the legitimate brother Tupac Amaru, both remaining in Vilcapampa.

Paullu Tupac Yupanqui, the next brother of Manco Inca, was baptized with the name of Cristóval. He accompanied Almagro in his expedition to Chile, and was with young Almagro at the battle of Chupas. Eventually he was allowed to fix his residence on the Colcampata of Cuzco, at the foot of the fortress, and by the side of the church of San Cristóval. From the terrace of the Colcampata there is a glorious view with the snowy peak of Vilcañota in the far distance. Paullu died in May, 1549, and was succeeded on the Colcampata by his son Carlos Inca. He had two other sons named Felipe and Bartolomé. From the latter was descended the late Archdeacon of Cuzco, Dr Justo Salmaraura Inca.

Titu Atauchi, the youngest son of Huayna Ccapac, had a son Alonso.

The princesses, daughters of Huayna Ccapac and sisters of Manco and Paullu, were Beatriz Ñusta, married first to Martin de Mustincia, and secondly to Diego Hernandez of Talavera; Leonor Ñusta, the wife of Juan de Balsa, who was killed at the battle of Chupas on the side of young Almagro, secondly of Francisco de Villacastin: Francisca Ñusta, niece of Huayna Ccapac, married to Juan de Collantes, and was great-grandmother of Bishop Piedrahita, the historian of

Nueva Granada: another Beatriz Ñusta married Mancio Sierra de Leguisano, the generous defender of the natives; and Inez Ñusta married first Francisco Pizarro and had a daughter Francisca, who has descendants, and secondly to Francisco Ampuero. Angelina, daughter of Atahualpa, was married to Juan de Betanzos, the author and Quichua scholar. The brother of Huayna Ccapac, named Hualpa Tupac Yupanqui, had a daughter, Isabel Ñusta Yupanqui, the wife of Garcilasso de la Vega, and mother of the Inca Garcilasso de la Vega[10], the historian, author of the Comentarios Reales.

[Note 10: The Inca Garcilasso was a third cousin of the regicide Viceroy Toledo. Their great grandfathers were brothers.]

This then was the position of the Inca family when the Viceroy, Francisco de Toledo, came to Cuzco in 1571. Cusi Titu Yupanqui and Tupac Amaru, sons of the Inca Manco were in the mountains of Vilcapampa, the former maintaining his independence. Carlos Inca, son of Paullu, was baptized, and living on the Colcampata at Cuzco with his wife Maria de Esquivel. Seven Inca princesses had married Spaniards, most of them living at Cuzco with their husbands and children.

The events, connected with the Inca family, which followed on the arrival of the Viceroy Toledo at Cuzco, will be found fully described in this volume. It need only be stated here that the inexorable tyrant, having got the innocent young prince Tupac Amaru into his power, resolved to put him to death. The native population was overwhelmed with grief. The Spaniards were horrified. They entreated that the lad might be sent to Spain to be judged by the King. The heads of religious orders and other ecclesiastics went down on their knees. Nothing could move the obstinate narrow-minded Viceroy. The deed was done.

When too late Toledo seems to have had some misgivings. The judicial murder took place in December, 1571. The history of the Incas was finished in March, 1572. Yet there is no mention of the death of Tupac Amaru. For all that appears he might have been still in Vilcapampa. Nevertheless the tidings reached Philip II, and the Viceroy's conduct was not approved.

There was astonishing audacity on the part of Toledo, in basing arguments on the alleged cruelty and tyranny of the Incas, when the man was actually red-handed with the blood of an innocent youth, and engaged in the tyrannical persecution of his relations and the hideous torture of his followers. His arguments made no impression on the mind of Philip II. The King even showed some favour to the children of Tupac Amaru by putting them in the succession to the Marquisate of Oropesa. In the Inca pedigrees Toledo is called "el execrable regicidio." When he presented himself on his return from Peru the King angrily exclaimed: "Go away to your house; for I sent you to serve kings; and you went to kill kings[11]."

[Note 11: "Idos a vuestra casa, que yo os envie a servir reyes; y vos fuiste a matar reyes."]

All his faithful services as a legislator and a statesman could not atone for this cruel judicial murder in the eyes of his sovereign. He went back to his house a disgraced and broken-hearted man, and died soon afterwards.

The history of the Incas by Sarmiento is followed, in this volume, by a narrative of the execution of Tupac Amaru and of the events leading to it, by an eye-witness, the Captain Baltasar de Ocampo. It has been translated from a manuscript in the British Museum.

The narrative of Ocampo, written many years after the event, is addressed to the Viceroy Marquis of Montes Claros. Its main object was to give an account of the province of Vilcapampa, and to obtain some favours for the Spanish settlers there.

Vilcapampa is a region of very special historical and geographical interest, and it is one of which very little is known. It is a mountainous tract of country, containing the lofty range of Vilcacunca and several fertile valleys, between the rivers Apurimac and Vilcamayu, to the north of Cuzco. The mountains rise abruptly from the valley of the Vilcamayu below Ollantay-tampu, where the bridge of Chuqui-chaca opened upon paths leading up into a land of enchantment. No more lovely mountain scenery can be found on this earth. When Manco Inca escaped from the Spaniards he took refuge in Vilcapampa, and established his court and government there. The Sun temple, the convent of virgins, and the other institutions of the Incas at Cuzco, were transferred to this mountain fastness. Even handsome edifices were erected. Here the Incas continued to maintain their independence for 35 years.

Ocampo opens his story with a very interesting account of the baptism of Melchior Carlos, son of Carlos Inca, who had become a Christian, and lived in the palace on the Colcampata at Cuzco. He then describes the events which culminated in the capture, of the Inca Tupac Amaru, and gives a pathetic and touching account of the judicial murder of that ill-fated young prince. Ocampo was an actor in these events and an eye-witness. The rest of his narrative consists of reminiscences of occurrences in Vilcapampa after it was occupied by the Spaniards. He owned property there, and was a settler holding official posts. He tells of the wealth and munificence of a neighbour. He gives the history of an expedition into the forests to the northward, which will form material for the history of these expeditions when it is written. He tells the story of an insurrection among the negro labourers, and complains of the spiritual destitution of his adopted land. He finally returns to Cuzco and gives an account of a very magnificent pageant and tilting match. But this story should have preceded the mournful narrative of the fate of Tupac Amaru; for the event took place at the time of the baptism of Melchior Carlos, and before the Viceroy Toledo became a regicide. Ocampo's story is that of an honest old soldier, inclined to be garrulous, but an eye-witness of some most interesting events in the history of Peru.

I think it is an appropriate sequel to the history by Sarmiento, because it supplies material for judging whether the usurpation and tyranny were on the side of the Incas or of their accuser.

THE SECOND PART OF THE GENERAL HISTORY CALLED "INDICA" WHICH WAS COMPOSED BY THE CAPTAIN PEDRO SARMIENTO DE GAMBOA BY ORDER OF THE MOST EXCELLENT LORD DON FRANCISCO DE TOLEDO VICEROY GOVERNOR AND CAPTAIN-GENERAL OF THE KINGDOMS OF PERU AND MAYOR-DOMO OF THE ROYAL HOUSEHOLD OF CASTILLE

1572

TO HIS SACRED CÆSARIAN MAJESTY THE KING, DON FELIPE, OUR LORD.

Among the excellencies, O sovereign and catholic Philip, that are the glorious decorations of princes, placing them on the highest pinnacle of estimation, are, according to the father of Latin eloquence, generosity, kindness, and liberality. And as the Roman Consuls held this to be the principal praise of their glory, they had this title curiously sculptured in marble on the Quirinal and in the forum of Trajan—-"Most powerful gift in a Prince is liberality[12]." For this kings who desired much to be held dear by their own people and to be feared by strangers, were incited to acquire the name of liberal. Hence that royal sentence became immortal "It is right for kings to give." As this was a quality much valued among the Greeks, the wise Ulysses, conversing with

Antinous[13], King of the Phæacians, said——"You are something like a king, for you know how to give, better than others." Hence it is certain that liberality is a good and necessary quality of kings.

[Note 12: "Primum signum nobilitatis est liberalitas."]

[Note 13: Alcinous.]

I do not pretend on this ground, most liberal monarch, to insinuate to your Majesty the most open frankness, for it would be very culpable on my part to venture to suggest a thing which, to your Majesty, is so natural that you would be unable to live without it. Nor will it happen to so high minded and liberal a lord and king, what befell the Emperor Titus who, remembering once, during supper time, that he had allowed one day to pass without doing some good, gave utterance to this laudable animadversion of himself. "O friends! I have lost a day[14]." For not only does your Majesty not miss a day, but not even an hour, without obliging all kinds of people with benefits and most gracious liberality. The whole people, with one voice, says to your Majesty what Virgil sang to Octavianus Augustus:

"Nocte pluit tota, redeunt spectacula mane,
Divisum imperium cum Jove Cæsar habet."

[Note 14: "Amici! diem perdidi." Suetonius.]

But what I desire to say is that for a king who complies so well with the obligation of liberality, and who gives so much, it is necessary that he should possess much; for nothing is so suitable for a prince as possessions and riches for his gifts and liberalities, as Tully says, as well as to acquire glory. For it is certain, as we read in Sallust that "in a vast empire there is great glory[15]"; and in how much it is greater, in so much it treats of great things. Hence the glory of a king consists in his possessing many vassals, and the abatement of his glory is caused by the diminution of the number of his subjects.

[Note 15: Proem of Catiline.]

Of this glory, most Christian king, God Almighty gives you so large a share in this life that all the enemies of the holy catholic church of Christ our Lord tremble at your exalted name; whence you most justly deserve to be named the strength of the church. As the treasure which God granted that your ancestors should spend, with such holy magnanimity, on worthy and holy deeds, in the extirpation of heretics, in driving the accursed Saracens out of Spain, in building churches, hospitals and monasteries, and in an infinite number of other works of charity and justice, with the zeal of zealous fathers of their country, not only entitled them to the most holy title of catholics, but the most merciful and almighty God, whom they served with all their hearts, saw fit to commence repayment with temporal goods, in the present age. It is certain that "He who grants celestial rewards does not take away temporal blessings[16]," so that they earned more than the mercies they received. This was the grant to them of the evangelical office, choosing them from among all the kings of this world as the evangelizers of his divine word in the most remote and unknown lands of those blind and barbarous gentiles. We now call those lands the Indies of Castille, because through the ministry of that kingdom they will be put in the way of salvation, God himself being the true pilot. He made clear and easy the dark and fearful Atlantic sea which had been an awful portent to the most ancient Argives, Athenians, Egyptians, and Phoenicians, and what is more to the proud Hercules, who, having come to Cadiz from the east, and seen the wide Atlantic sea, he thought this was the end of the world and that there was no more land. So he set up his columns with this inscription "Ultra Gades nil" or "Beyond Cadiz there is nothing." But as human knowledge is ignorance in the sight of God, and the force of the world but weakness in his presence, it was very easy, with the power of the Almighty and of your grandparents, to break and scatter the mists and difficulties of the enchanted ocean. Laughing with good reason at Alcides and his inscription, they discovered the Indies which were very populous in souls to whom the road to heaven could be shown. The Indies are also most abundant in all kinds of inestimable treasures, with which the heavy expenses were repaid to them, and yet remained the richest princes in the world, and thus continued to exercise their holy and Christian liberality until death. By reason of this most famous navigation, and new and marvellous discovery, they amended the inscription on the columns of Hercules, substituting "Plus ultra" for "Ultra Gades nil"; the meaning was, and with much truth, that further on there are many lands. So this inscription, "Plus ultra," remained on the blazon of the arms and insignia of the Indies of Castille.

[Note 16: From the poem of Coelius Sedulius, a Christian poet who flourished about A.D. 450. The passage is—"Hostis Herodes impie Christum venire quod timeo? Non eripit mortalia qui regna dat coelestia." (Note by Dr Peitschmann.)]

As there are few who are not afflicted by the accursed hunger for gold, and as good successes are food for an enemy, the devil moved the bosoms of some powerful princes with the desire to take part in this great business. Alexander VI, the Vicar of Jesus Christ, considering that this might give rise to impediments in preaching the holy evangel to the barbarous idolaters, besides other evils which might be caused, desired of his own proper motion, without any petition from the catholic kings, by authority of Almighty God, to give, and he gave and conceded for ever, the islands and main lands which were then discovered and which might hereafter be discovered within the limits and demarcation of 180° of longitude, which is half the world, with all the dominions, rights, jurisdictions and belongings, prohibiting the navigation and trading in those lands from whatever cause, to the other princes, kings, and emperors from the year 1493, to prevent many inconveniences.

But as the devil saw that this door was shut, which he had begun to open to introduce by it dissensions and disturbances, he tried to make war by means of the very soldiers who resisted him, who were the same preachers. They began to make a difficulty about the right and title which the kings of Castille had over these lands. As your invincible father was very jealous in matters touching his conscience, he ordered this point to be examined, as closely as possible, by very learned doctors who, according to the report which was given out, were indirect and doubtful in their conclusions. They gave it as their opinion that these Incas, who ruled in these kingdoms of Peru, were and are the true and natural lords of that land. This gave a handle to foreigners, as well catholics as heretics and other infidels, for throwing doubt on the right which the kings of Spain claim and have claimed to the Indies. Owing to this the Emperor Don Carlos of glorious memory was on the point of abandoning them, which was what the enemy of the faith of Christ wanted, that he might regain the possession of the souls which he had kept in blindness for so many ages.

All this arose owing to want of curiosity on the part of the governors in those lands, at that time, who did not use the diligence necessary for ascertaining the truth, and also owing to certain reports of the Bishop of Chiapa who was moved to passion against certain conquerors in his bishoprick with whom he had persistent disputes, as I knew when I passed through Chiapa and Guatemala[17]. Though his zeal appears holy and estimable, he said things on the right to this country gained by the conquerors of it, which differ from the evidence and judicial proofs which have been seen and taken down by us, and from what we who have travelled over the Indies enquiring about these things, leisurely and without war, know to be the facts[18].

[Note 17: See the introduction to my Voyages of Sarmiento p. x.]

[Note 18: Sarmiento here refers to the efforts of Las Casas to protect the natives from the tyranny and cruelties of the Spanish settlers. He appears to have been in Guatemala when Las Casas arrived to take up his appointment as Bishop of Chiapas, and encountered hostility and obstruction from certain "conquistadores de su obispado," as Sarmiento calls them. On his return to Spain, the good Las Casas found that a certain Dr Sepulveda had written a treatise maintaining the right of Spain to subdue the natives by war. Las Casas put forward his Historia Apologetica in reply. A Junta of theologians was convoked at Valladolid in 1550, before which Sepulveda attacked and Las Casas defended the cause of the natives. Mr. Helps (Spanish conquest in America, vol. iv. Book xx. ch. 2) has given a lucid account of the controversy. Sarmiento is quite wrong in saying that Las Casas was ignorant of the history of Peru. The portion of his Historia Apologetica relating to Peru, entitled De las antiguas gentes del Peru, has been edited and published by Don Marcos Jimenez de la Espada in the "Coleccion de libros Españoles raros ó curiosos" (1892). It shows that Las Casas knew the works of Xeres, Astete, Cieza de Leon, Molina, and probably others; and that he had a remarkably accurate knowledge of Peruvian history.]

This chaos and confusion of ignorance on the subject being so spread over the world and rooted in the opinions of the best informed literary men in Christendom, God put it into the heart of your Majesty to send Don Francisco de Toledo, Mayor-domo of your royal household, as Viceroy of these kingdoms[19]. When he arrived, he found many things to do, and many things to amend. Without resting after the dangers and long voyages in two seas which he had suffered, he put the needful order into all the things undertook new and greater labours, such as no former viceroys or governors had undertaken or even thought of. His determination was to travel over this most rugged country himself, to make a general visitation of it, during which, though it is not finished, it is certain that he has remedied many and very great faults and abuses in the teaching and ministry of the Christian doctrine, giving holy and wise advice to its ministers that they should perform their offices as becomes the service of God, and the discharge of your royal conscience, reducing the people to congregations of villages formed on suitable and healthy sites which had formerly been on crags and rocks where they were neither taught nor received spiritual instruction. In such places they lived and died like wild savages, worshipping idols as in the time of their Inca tyrants and of their blind heathenism. Orders were given to stop their public drinking bouts, their concubinage and worship of their idols and devils, emancipating and freeing them from the tyrannies, of their curacas, and finally giving them a rational life, which was before that of brutes in their manner of loading them as such.

[Note 19: Don Francisco de Toledo was Viceroy of Peru, from Nov. 16th, 1569, to Sept. 28th, 1581, and in some respects a remarkable man. He was a younger son of the third Count of Oropesa who had a common ancestor with the Dukes of Alva. His mother was Maria de Figueroa daughter of the Count of Feria. Through her he was directly descended from the first Duke of Alva. He was a first cousin of that Duke of Feria who made a love match with Jane Dormer, the friend and playmate of our Edward VI. Moreover Don Francisco was a third cousin of Charles V. Their great grandmothers were sisters, daughters of Fadrique Henriquez, the Admiral of Castille.

This Viceroy was advanced in years. He held the appointment of a Mayor-domo at the court of Philip II, and another brother Juan was Ambassador at Rome. The Viceroy Toledo came to Peru with the Inquisition, which proved as great a nuisance to him as it was a paralyzing source of terror to his people. He was a man of extraordinary energy and resolution, and was devoted heart and soul to the public service. Sarmiento does not speak too highly of his devotion to duty in undertaking a personal visit to every part of his government. He was a most prolific legislator, founding his rules, to some extent, on the laws of the Incas. He was shrewd but narrow minded and heartless; and his judicial murder of the young Inca, Tupac Amaru, has cast an indelible stain on his memory.

Such a man could have no chance in an attack on the sound arguments of Las Casas.

There is a picture which depicts the outward appearance of the Viceroy Toledo. A tall man with round stooping shoulders, in a suit of black velvet with the green cross of Alcantara embroidered on his cloak. A gloomy sallow face, with aquiline nose, high forehead and piercing black eyes too close together. The face is shaded by a high beaver hat, while one hand holds a sword, and the other rests on a table.]

The work done by your Viceroy is such that the Indians are regenerated, and they call him loudly their protector and guardian, and your Majesty who sent him, they call their father. So widely has the news spread of the benefits he has conferred and is still conferring, that the wild warlike Indians in many contiguous provinces, holding themselves to be secure under his word and safe conduct, have come to see and communicate with him, and have promised obedience spontaneously to your Majesty. This has happened in the Andes of Xauxa, near Pilcocanti, and among the Mañaries and Chunchos to the east of Cuzco. These were sent back to their homes, grateful and attached to your royal service, with the presents he gave them and the memory of their reception.

Among Christians, it is not right to take anything without a good title, yet that which your Majesty has to these parts, though more holy and more honourable than that which any other kings in the world have for any of their possessions, has suffered detriment, as I said before, in the consciences of many learned men and others, for want of correct information. The Viceroy proposes to do your Majesty a most signal service in this matter, besides the performance of all the other duties of which he has charge. This is to give a secure and quiet harbour to your royal conscience against the tempests raised even by your own natural subjects, theologians and other literary men, who have expressed serious opinions on the subject, based on incorrect information. Accordingly, in his general visitation, which he is making personally throughout the kingdom, he has verified from the root and established by a host of witnesses examined with the greatest diligence and care, taken from among the principal old men of the greatest ability and authority in the kingdom, and even those who pretend to have an interest in it from being relations and descendants of the Incas, the terrible, inveterate and horrible tyranny of the Incas, being the tyrants who ruled in these kingdoms of Peru, and the curacas who governed the districts. This will undeceive all those in the world who think that the Incas were legitimate sovereigns, and that the curacas were natural lords of the land. In order that your Majesty may, with the least trouble and the most pleasure, be informed, and the rest, who are of a contrary opinion, be undeceived, I was ordered by the Viceroy Don Francisco de Toledo, whom I follow and serve in this general visitation, to take this business in hand, and write a history of the deeds of the twelve Incas of this land, and of the origin of the people, continuing the narrative to the end. This I have done with all the research and diligence that was required, as your Majesty will see in the course of the perusal and by the ratification of witnesses. It will certify to the truth of the worst and most inhuman tyranny of these Incas and of their curacas who are not and never were original lords of the soil, but were placed there by Tupac Inca Yupanqui, [the greatest, the most atrocious and harmful tyrant of them all]. The curacas were and still are great tyrants appointed by other great and violent tyrants, as will clearly and certainly appear in the history; so that the tyranny is proved, as well as that the Incas were strangers in Cuzco, and that they had seized the valley of Cuzco, and all the rest of their territory from Quito to Chile by force of arms, making themselves Incas without the consent or election of the natives.

Besides this, there are their tyrannical laws and customs. [It will be understood that your Majesty has a specially true and holy title to these kingdoms of Peru, because your Majesty and your most sacred ancestors stopped the sacrifices of innocent men, the eating of human flesh, the accursed sin, the promiscuous concubinage with sisters and mothers, the abominable use of beasts, and their wicked and accursed customs[20].] For from each one God demands an account of his neighbour, and this duty specially appertains to princes, and above all to your Majesty. Only for this may war be made and prosecuted by the right to put a stop to the deeds of tyrants. Even if they had been true and natural lords of the soil, it would be lawful to remove them and introduce a new government, because man may rightly be punished for these sins against nature, though the native community has not been opposed to such practices nor desires to be avenged, as innocent, by the Spaniards. For in this case they have no right to deliver themselves and their children over to death, and they should be forced to observe natural laws, as we are taught by the Archbishop of Florence, Innocent, supported by Fray, Francisco de Victoria in his work on the title to the Indies. So that by this title alone, without counting many others, your Majesty has the most sufficient and legitimate right to the Indies, better than any other prince in the world has to any lordship whatever. For, whether more or less concealed or made known, in all the lands that have been discovered in the two seas of your Majesty, north and south, this general breaking of the law of nature has been found.

[Note 20: For a contradiction of these slanders by an impartial witness see Cieza de Leon, ii. p. 78.]

By this same title your Majesty may also, without scruple, order the conquest of those islands of the archipelago of "Nombre de Jesus," vulgarly but incorrectly called the Solomon Isles, of which I gave notice and personally discovered in the year 1567; although it was for the General Alvaro de Mendaña; and many others which are in the same South Sea[21]. I offer myself to your Majesty to discover and settle these islands, which will make known and facilitate all the commercial navigation, with the favour of God, by shorter routes. I offer much, well do I see it, but I trust in almighty God with whose favour, I believe I can do what I say in your royal service. The talent which God has given me leads me to aspire to the accomplishment of these achievements, and does not demand of me a strict account, and I believe that I shall comply with what will be required, for never did I so wish to achieve anything. Your Majesty sees and does not lose what other kings desire and hold by good fortune. This makes me speak so freely of my desire to die in your service in which I have laboured since my childhood, and under what circumstances others may say.

[Note 21: See my introduction to the Voyages of Sarmiento, pp. xiii—xvii.]

Believing that, in writing this present history, I have not done a less but a greater service than all the rest, I obeyed your Viceroy who made me undertake it. Your Majesty will read it many times because, besides that the reading of it is pleasant, your Majesty will take a great interest in the matters of conscience and of administration of which it treats. I call this the Second Part, because it is to be preceded by the geographical description of all these lands, which will form the First Part. This will result in great clearness for the comprehension of the establishment of governments, bishopricks, new settlements, and of discoveries, and will obviate the inconveniences formerly caused by the want of such knowledge. Although the First Part ought to precede this one in time, it is not sent to your Majesty because it is not finished, a great part of it being derived from information collected during the general visitation. Suffice that it will be best in quality, though not in time. After this Second Part will be sent a Third Part on the times of the evangel. All this I have to finish by order of the Viceroy Don Francisco de Toledo. May your Majesty receive my work with the greatest and most favourable attention, as treating of things that will be of service to God and to your Majesty and of great profit to my nation; and may our Lord preserve the sacred catholic and royal person of your Majesty, for the repair and increase of the catholic Church of Jesus Christ.

From Cuzco. The 4th of March, 1572.

Your catholic royal Majesty

from the least vassal of your Majesty

The Captain

Pedro Sarmiento de Gamboa.

I.DIVISION OF THE HISTORY.

This general history of which I took charge by order of Don Francisco de Toledo, Viceroy of these kingdoms of Peru, will be divided into three Parts. The First will be the natural history of these lands, being a particular description of them. It will contain accounts of the marvellous works of nature, and other things of great profit and interest. I am now finishing it, that it may be sent to your Majesty after this, though it ought to have come before it. The Second and Third Parts treat of the people of these kingdoms and of their deeds in the following order. In the Second Part, which is the present one, the most ancient and first peoplers of this land will be discussed in general, and then, descending to particulars, I shall describe [the terrible and inveterate tyranny of] the Ccapac Incas of these kingdoms, down to the end and death of Huascar, the last of the Incas. The Third and Last Part will treat of the times of the Spaniards, and of their notable deeds in the discovery and settlement of this kingdom and others adjoining it, with the captains, governors, and viceroys who have ruled here, down to the present year 1572.

II.THE ANCIENT DIVISION OF THE LAND.

When historians wish to write, in an orderly way, of the world or some part of it, they generally first describe the situation containing it, which is the land, before they deal with what it contains, which is the population, to avoid the former in the historical part. If this is so in ancient and well known works, it is still more desirable that in treating of new and strange lands, like these, of such vast extent, a task which I have undertaken, the same order should be preserved. This will not only supply interesting information but also, which is more to be desired, it will be useful for navigation and new discoveries, by which God our Lord may be served, the territories of the crown of Spain extended, and Spaniards enriched and respected. As I have not yet finished the particular description of this land, which will contain everything relating to geography and the works of nature minutely dealt with, in this volume I shall only offer a general summary, following the most ancient authors, to recall the remains of those lands which are now held to be new and previously unknown, and of their inhabitants.

The land, which we read of as having existed in the first and second age of the world, was divided into five parts. The three continents, of which geographers usually write, Asia, Africa, and Europe, are divided by the river Tanais, the river Nile, and the Mediterranean Sea, which Pomponius calls "our" sea. Asia is divided from Europe by the river Tanais[22], now called Silin, and from Africa by the Nile, though Ptolemy divides it by the Red Sea and isthmus of the desert of Arabia Deserta. Africa is divided from Europe by "our" sea, commencing at the strait of Gibraltar and ending with the Lake of Meotis. The other two parts are thus divided. One was called, and still ought to be called, Catigara[23] in the Indian Sea, a very extensive land now distinct from Asia. Ptolemy describes it as being, in his time and in the time of Alexander the Great, joined on to Asia in the direction of Malacca. I shall treat of this in its place, for it contains many and very precious secrets, and an infinity of souls, to whom the King our Lord may announce the holy catholic faith that they may be saved, for this is the object of his Majesty in these new lands of barbarous idolatry. The fifth part is or was called the Atlantic Island, as famous as extensive, and which exceeded all the others, each one by itself, and even some joined together. The inhabitants of it and their description will be treated of, because this is the land, or at least part of it, of these western Indies of Castille.

[Note 22: The Don.]

[Note 23: Marinus of Tyre, quoted by Ptolemy, gave an enormous extension to eastern Asia, and placed the region he called Catigara far to the S.E. of it. Catigara was described by Marinus of Tyre as an emporium and important place of trade. It is not mentioned in the Periplus of the Erythræan Sea.]

III.

DESCRIPTION OF THE ANCIENT ATLANTIC ISLAND.

The cosmographers do not write of this ancient Atlantic Island because there was no memory, when they wrote, of its very rich commercial prosperity in the second, and perhaps in the first age. But from what the divine Plato tells us and from the vestiges we see which agree with what we read, we can not only say where it was and where parts of it were, as seen in our time, but we can describe it almost exactly, its grandeur and position. This is the truth, and the same Plato affirms it as true, in the Timæus, where he gives its truthful and marvellous history.

We will speak first of its situation, and then of its inhabitants. It is desirable that the reader should give his attention because, although it is very ancient history, it is so new to the ordinary teaching of cosmography that it may cause such surprise as to raise doubts of the story, whence may arise a want of appreciation.

From the words which Plato refers to Solon, the wisest of the seven of Greece, and which Solon had heard with attention from the most learned Egyptian priest in the city called Delta, we learn that this Atlantic Island was larger than Asia and Africa together, and that the eastern end of this immense island was near the strait which we now call of Gibraltar. In front of the mouth of the said strait, the island had a port with a narrow entrance; and Plato says that the island was truly continental. From it there was a passage by the sea, which surrounded it, to many other neighbouring islands, and to the main land of Europe and Africa. In this island there were kings of great and admirable power who ruled over that and many adjacent islands as well as the greater part of Europe and Africa, up to the confines of Egypt, of which I shall treat presently. The extent of the island was from the south, where were the highest mountains, to the north. The mountains exceeded in extent any that now exist, as well in their forests, as in height, and in beauty. These are the words of Plato in describing the situation of this most richly endowed and delightful Atlantic Island. It now remains for me to do my duty, which is to explain what has been said more clearly and from it to deduce the situation of the island.

From what Plato says that this island had a port near the mouth of the strait of the pillars of

Hercules, that it was larger than Asia and Africa together, and that it extended to the south, I gather three things clearly towards the understanding of all that invites attention. The first is that the Atlantic Island began less than two leagues from the mouth of the strait, if more it was only a little more. The coast of the island then turned north close to that of Spain, and was joined to the island of Cadiz or Gadiz, or Caliz, as it is now called. I affirm this for two reasons, one by authority and the other by conjectural demonstration. The authority is that Plato in his Critias, telling how Neptune distributed the sovereignty of the island among his ten sons, said that the second son was called in the mother tongue "Gadirum," which in Greek we call "Eumelo." To this son he gave the extreme parts of the island near the columns of Hercules, and from his name the place was called Gadiricum which is Caliz. By demonstration we see, and I have seen with my own eyes, more than a league out at sea and in the neighbourhood of the island of Caliz, under the water, the remains of very large edifices of a cement which is almost imperishable[24], an evident sign that this island was once much larger, which corroborates the narrative of Critias in Plato. The second point is that the Atlantic Island was larger than Asia and Africa. From this I deduce its size, which is incredible or at least immense. It would give the island 2300 leagues of longitude, that is from east to west. For Asia has 1500 leagues in a straight line from Malacca which is on its eastern front, to the boundary of Egypt; and Africa has 800 leagues from Egypt to the end of the Atlantic mountains or "Montes Claros" facing the Canary Islands; which together make 2300 leagues of longitude. If the island was larger it would be more in circuit. Round the coast it would have 7100 leagues, for Asia is 5300 and Africa 2700 leagues in circuit, a little more or less, which together makes 7100 leagues, and it is even said that it was more.

[Note 24: Dr Peitschmann quotes from Juan Bautista Suarez de Salazar, Grandezas y antigüedades de la isla y ciudad de Cadiz (Cadiz, 1610)—"That which all those who traverse the sea affirm was that to the south, the water being clear, there is seen beneath it at a distance of a league, ruins of edifices which are good evidence that the ocean has gained upon the land in this part." He refers also to a more recent history of Cadiz and its province by Adolfo de Castro (1858), and to the five first books of the General Chronicle of Spain of Florian de Ocampo, 1552 (lib. ii. cap. II).]

Having considered the measurement of its great size we come to the third point, which is the true position over which this great island extended. Plato says that the position of the island extended to the south; opposite to the north. From this we should understand that, the front conterminous with Spain from the strait of Gibraltar to Cadiz thence extended westward, making a curve along the coast of Barbary or Africa, but very close to it, between west and south, which is what sailors call south-west. For if it was opposite to north, which is between east and north, called north-east, it must necessarily have its direction in the said south-west, west-south-west, or south-south-west. It would include and incorporate the Canary Islands which, according to this calculation, would be part of it, and from thence the land trended south-west. As regards the south, it would extend rather more to the south and south-south-west, finally following the route by which we go when we sail from Spain to the Indies, forming a continent or main land with these western Indies of Castille, joining on to them by the parts stretching south-west, and west-south-west, a little more or less from the Canaries. Thus there was sea on one side and on the other of this land, that is on the north and south, and the Indies united with it, and they were all one. The proof of this is that if the Atlantic Island had 2300 leagues of longitude, and the distance of Cadiz to the mouth of the river Marañon or Orellana and Trinidad, on the coast of Brazil, is, not more than 1000, 900, or 1100 leagues, being the part where this land joined to America, it clearly appears that, to complete the complement of 2300 leagues, we have to include in the computation all the rest of the land from the mouth of the Marañon and Brazil to the South Sea, which is what they now call America. Following this course it would come to Coquimbo. Counting what is still wanting, this would be much less than 2300 leagues. Measuring the circumference, the island was more than 7100 leagues round, because that is about the circumference of Asia and Africa by their coasts. If this land is joined to the other, which in fact it was in conformity with the description, it would have a much greater circuit, for even now these parts of the western Indies, measured by compass, and latitude, have more than 7100 leagues.

From all this it may be inferred that the Indies of Castille formed a continent with the Atlantic Island, and consequently that the same Atlantic Island, which extended from Cadiz over the sea we traverse to the Indies, and which all cosmographers call the Atlantic Ocean because the Atlantic Island was in it, over which we now navigate, was land in ancient times. Finally we shall relate the sequel, first giving an account of the sphere at that time and of the inhabitants.

IV.FIRST INHABITANTS OF THE WORLD AND PRINCIPALLY OF THE ATLANTIC ISLAND.

Having described the four parts of the world, for of Catigara, which is the fifth, we shall not speak except in its place which the ancients assigned to it, it will be right to come to the races which peopled them. All of which I have to treat has to be personal and heathen history. The chief value and perfection of history consists in its accuracy, thoroughly sifting each event, verifying the times and periods of what happened so that no doubt may remain of what passed. It is in this way that I desire to write the truth in so far as my ability enables me to do so respecting a thing so ancient as the first peopling of these new lands. I wish, for the better illustration of the present history, to precede it with the foundations that cannot be denied, counting the time in conformity with the chronology of the Hebrews in the days before our Saviour Jesus Christ, and the times after his most holy nativity according to the counting used by our mother the holy church, not making account of the calculations of Chaldean or Egyptian interpreters.

Thus, passing over the first age from Adam to the Deluge, which covers 1656 years, we will begin from the second age, which is that of the patriarch Noah, second universal father of mortals. The divine scriptures show us that eight persons were saved from the flood, in the ark. Noah and his wife Terra or Vesta, named from the first fire lighted by crystal for the first sacrifice as Berosus would have; and his three sons to wit, Cam and his wife Cataflua, Sem and his wife Prusia or Persia, Japhet and his wife Fun a, as we read in the register of the chronicles. The names of some of these people remain, and to this day we can see clearly whence they were derived, as the Hebrews from Heber, the Assyrians from Amur, but most of them have been so changed that human intelligence is insufficient to investigate by this way. Besides the three sons, Noah had others after the flood.

The descendants of these men having multiplied and become very numerous, Noah divided the world among his first sons that they might people it, and then embarked on the Euxine Sea as we gather from Xenophon. The giant Noah then navigated along the Mediterranean Sea, as Filon says and Annius repeats, dividing the whole land among his sons. He gave it in charge to Sem to people Asia from the Nile to the eastern Indies, with some of the sons he got after the flood. To Cam he gave Africa from the Rinocoruras to the straits of Gibraltar with some more of the sons. Europe was chosen for Japhet to people with the rest of the sons begotten after the flood, who were all the sons of Tuscan, whence descend the Tadescos, Alemanes, and the nations adjacent to them.

In this voyage Noah founded some towns and colonies on the shores of the Mediterranean Sea, and remained in them for ten years, until 112 years after the universal deluge. He ordered his daughter Araxa to remain in Armenia where the ark rested, with her husband and children, to people that country. Then he, with the rest of his companions, went to Mesopotamia and settled. There Nembrot was raised up for king, of the descendants of Cam. This Nembrot, says Berosus, built Babylon 130 years after the flood. The sons of Sem elected for their king, Jektan, son of Heber. Those of Japhet chose Fenec for their king, called Assenes by Moses. There were 300,000 men under him only 310 years after the deluge. Each king, with his companions, set out to people the part of the world chosen for them by the patriarch Noah. It is to be noted that, although Noah divided the parts of the world among his three sons and their descendants, many of them did not keep to the boundaries. For some of one lineage settled on the lands of another brother. Nembrot, being of the line of Cam, remained in the parts of Sem, and many others were mixed together in the same way.

Thus the three parts of the world were peopled by these and their descendants, of whom I do not propose to treat in detail, for our plan is to proceed in our narrative until we come to the inhabitants of the Atlantic Island, the subject of this history. This was so near Spain that, according to the common fame, Caliz used to be so close to the main land in the direction of the port of Santa Maria, that a plank would serve as a bridge to pass from the island to Spain. So that no one can doubt that the inhabitants of Spain, Jubal and his descendants, peopled that land, as well as the inhabitants of Africa which was also near. Hence it was called the Atlantic Island from having been peopled by Atlas, the giant and very wise astrologer who first settled Mauritania now called Barbary, as Godefridus and all the chronicles teach us. This Atlas was the son of Japhet by the nymph Asia, and grandson of Noah. For this there is no authority except the above, corroborated by the divine Plato as I began by explaining, and it will be necessary to seek his help to give the reader such evidence as merits belief respecting the inhabitants of this Atlantic Island.

V. INHABITANTS OF THE ATLANTIC ISLAND.

We have indicated the situation of the Atlantic Island and those who, in conformity with the general peopling of the world, were probably its first inhabitants, namely the early Spaniards and the first Mauritanian vassals of the King Atlas. This wonderful history was almost forgotten in ancient times, Plato alone having preserved it, as has already been related in its place, and which should again be consulted for what remains. Plato, in Critias, says that to Neptune's share came the Atlantic Island, and that he had ten sons. He divided the whole island amongst them, which before and in his time was called the empire of the floating islands, as Volaterranius tells us. It was divided by Neptune into ten regions or kingdoms. The chief one, called Venus, he gave to his eldest son named Atlantis, and appointed him sovereign of the whole island; which consequently took the name of Atlantica, and the sea Atlantic, a name which it retains to this day. The second son, named Gadirun, received the part which lies nearest to Spain and which is now Caliz. To the third son Neptune gave a share. His name was Amferes, the fourth's Eutoctenes, the seventh's Alusipo, the eighth's Mestores, the ninth's Azaen, the tenth's Diaprepem. These and their descendants reigned for many ages, holding the lordships, by the sea, of many other islands, which could not have been other than Hayti, which we call Santo Domingo, Cuba and others, also peopled by emigrants from the Atlantic Island. They also held sway over Africa as far as Egypt, and over Europe to Tirrenia and Italy.

The lineage of Atlas extended in a grand succession of generations, and his kingdom was ruled in succession by the firstborns. They possessed such a copious supply of riches that none of the natives had seen it all, and that no new comers could realise it. This land abounded in all that is necessary for sustaining human life, pasture, timber, drugs, metals, wild beasts and birds, domestic animals including a great number of elephants, most fragrant perfumes, liquors, flowers, fruits, wine, and all the vegetables used for food, many dates, and other things for presents. That island produced all things in great profusion. In ancient times it was sacred, beautiful, admirable and fertile, as well as of vast extent. In it were extensive kingdoms, sumptuous temples, palaces calling forth great admiration, as is seen from the relation of Plato respecting the metropolis of the island which exceeded Babylon, Troy, or Rome, with all their rich buildings, curious and well-constructed forts, and even the seven wonders of the world concerning which the ancients sing so much. In the chief city of this empire there was a port to which so many ships and merchants resorted from all parts, that owing to the vast concourse a great and continual noise caused the residents to be thunderstruck. The number of these Atlantics ready for war was so great that in the capital city alone they had an ordinary garrison of 60,000 soldiers, always distributed among farms, each farm measuring 100 furlongs. The rest inhabited the woods and other places, and were innumerable. They took to war 10,000 two-horse chariots each containing eight armed men, with six slingers and stone throwers on either side. For the sea they had 200,000 boats with four men in each, making 800,000 men for the sea-service alone. This was quite necessary owing to the great number of subject nations which had to be governed and kept in obedience.

The rest which Plato relates on this subject will be discussed in the sequel, for I now proceed to our principal point, which is to establish the conclusion that as these people carried their banners and trophies into Europe and Africa which are not contiguous, they must have overrun the Indies of Castille and peopled them, being part of the same main land. They used much policy in their rule. But at the end of many ages, by divine permission, and perhaps owing to their sins, it happened that a great and continuous earthquake, with an unceasing deluge, perpetual by day and night, opened the earth and swallowed up those warlike and ambitious Atlantic men. The Atlantic Island remained absorbed beneath that great sea, which from that cause continued to be unnavigable owing to the mud of the absorbed island in solution, a wonderful thing.

This special flood may be added to the five floods recorded by the ancients. These are the general one of Moses, the second in Egypt of which Xenophon makes mention, the third flood in Achaia of Greece in the time of Ogyges Atticus, described by Isidore as happening in the days of Jacob, the fourth in Thessaly in the time of Deucalion and Pyrrha, in the days of Moses according to Isidore, in 782 as given by Juan Annius. The fifth flood is mentioned by Xenophon as happening in Egypt in the time of Proteus. The sixth was this which destroyed so great a part of the Atlantic Island and sufficed so to separate the part that was left unsubmerged, that all mortals in Asia, Africa and Europe believed that all were drowned. Thus was lost the intercourse and commerce of the people of these parts with those of Europe and Africa, in such sort that all memory of them would have been lost, if it had not been for the Egyptians, preservers of the most ancient deeds of men and of nature. The destruction of the Atlantic Island, over at least 1000 leagues of longitude, was in the time when Aod[25] governed the people of Israel, 1320 years before Christ and 2162 years after the Creation, according to the Hebrews. I deduce this calculation from what Plato relates of the conversation between Solon and the Egyptian priest. For, according to all the chronicles, Solon lived in the time of Tarquinius Priscus the King of Rome, Josiah being King of Israel at Jerusalem, before Christ 610 years. From this period until the time when the Atlantics had put a blockade over the Athenians 9000 lunar years had passed

which, referred to solar years, make 869. All added together make the total given above. Very soon afterwards the deluge must have come, as it is said to have been in the time of Aod[25] or 748 years after the general deluge of Noah. This being so it is to be noted that the isle of Caliz, the Canaries, the Salvages, and Trinidad must have been parts of the absorbed land.
[Note 25: Ehud.]
It may be assumed that these very numerous nations of Atlantis were sufficient to people those other lands of the Western Indies of Castille. Other nations also came to them, and peopled some provinces after the above destruction. Strabo and Solinus say that Ulysses, after the fall of Troy, navigated westward to Lusitania, founded Lisbon, and, after it had been built, desired to try his fortune on the Atlantic Ocean by the way we now go to the Indies. He disappeared, and it was never afterwards known what had become of him. This is stated by Pero Anton Beuter, a noble Valencian historian and, as he mentions, this was the opinion of Dante Aligheri, the illustrious Florentine poet. Assuming this to be correct we may follow Ulysses from island to island until he came to Yucatan and Campeachy, part of the territory of New Spain. For those of that land have the Grecian bearing and dress of the nation of Ulysses, they have many Grecian words, and use Grecian letters. Of this I have myself seen many signs and proofs. Their name for God is "Teos" which is Greek, and even throughout New Spain they use the word "Teos" for God. I have also to say that in passing that way, I found that they anciently preserved an anchor of a ship, venerating it as an idol, and had a certain genesis in Greek, which should not be dismissed as absurd at first sight. Indeed there are a sufficient number of indications to support my conjecture concerning Ulysses. From thence all those provinces of Mexico, Tabasco, Xalisco, and to the north the Capotecas, Chiapas, Guatemalas, Honduras, Lasandones, Nicaraguas, Tlaguzgalpas, as far as Nicoya, Costa Rica, and Veragua.

Moreover Esdras recounts that those nations which went from Persia by the river Euphrates came to a land never before inhabited by the human race. Going down this river there was no way but by the Indian Sea to reach a land where there was no habitation. This could only have been Catigara, placed in 90° S. by Ptolemy, and according to the navigators sent by Alexander the Great, 40 days of navigation from Asia. This is the land which the describers of maps call the unknown land of the south, whence it is possible to go on settling people as far as the Strait of Magellan to the west of Catigara, and the Javas, New Guinea, and the islands of the archipelago of Nombre de Jesus which I, our Lord permitting, discovered in the South Sea in the year 1568, the unconquered Felipe II reigning as King of Spain and its dependencies by the demarcation of 180° of longitude.

It may thus be deduced that New Spain and its provinces were peopled by the Greeks, those of Catigara by the Jews, and those of the rich and most powerful kingdoms of Peru and adjacent provinces by the Atlantics who were descended from the primeval Mesopotamians and Chaldæans, peoplers of the world.

These, and other points with them, which cannot be discussed with brevity, are true historical reasons, of a quality worthy of belief, such as men of reason and letters may adopt respecting the peopling of these lands. When we come to consider attentively what these barbarians of Peru relate of their origin and of the tyrannical rule of the Incas Ccapacs, and the fables and extravagances they recount, the truth may be distinguished from what is false, and how in some of their fables they allude to true facts which are admitted and held by us as such. Therefore the reader should peruse with attention and read the most strange and racy history of barbarians that has, until now, been read of any political nation in the world.

VI.THE FABLE OF THE ORIGIN OF THESE BARBAROUS INDIANS OF PERU, ACCORDING TO THEIR BLIND OPINIONS.

As these barbarous nations of Indians were always without letters, they had not the means of preserving the monuments and memorials of their times, and those of their predecessors with accuracy and method. As the devil, who is always striving to injure the human race, found these unfortunates to be easy of belief and timid in obedience, he introduced many illusions, lies and frauds, giving them to understand that he had created them from the first, and afterwards, owing to their sins and evil deeds, he had destroyed them with a flood, again creating them and giving them food and the way to preserve it. By chance they formerly had some notice, passed down to them from mouth to mouth, which had reached them from their ancestors, respecting the truth of what happened in former times. Mixing this with the stories told them by the devil, and with other things which they changed, invented, or added, which may happen in all nations, they made up a pleasing salad, and in some things worthy of the attention of the curious who are accustomed to consider and discuss human ideas.

One thing must be noted among many others. It is that the stories which are here treated as fables, which they are, are held by the natives to be as true as we hold the articles of our faith, and as such they affirm and confirm them with unanimity, and swear by them. There are a few, however, who by the mercy of God are opening their eyes and beginning to see what is true and what is false respecting those things. But we have to write down what they say and not what we think about it in this part. We shall hear what they hold respecting their first age, [and afterwards we shall come to the inveterate and cruel tyranny of the Inca tyrants who oppressed these kingdoms of Peru for so long. All this is done by order of the most excellent Don Francisco de Toledo, Viceroy of these kingdoms]. I have collected the information with much diligence so that this history can rest on attested proofs from the general testimony of the whole kingdom, old and young, Incas and tributary Indians.

The natives of this land affirm that in the beginning, and before this world was created, there was a being called Viracocha. He created a dark world without sun, moon or stars. Owing to this creation he was named Viracocha Pachayachachi, which means "Creator of all things[26]."

[Note 26: Uiracocha (Viracocha) was the Creator. Garcilasso de la Vega pointed out the mistake of supposing that the word signified "foam of the sea" (ii. p. 16). He believed it to be a name, the derivation of which he did not attempt to explain. Blas Valera (i. p. 243) said the meaning was the "will and power of God"; not that this is the signification of the word, but by reason of the godlike qualities attributed to Him who was known by it. Cieza de Leon says that Tici-Uiracocha was God, Creator of heaven and earth: Acosta that to Tici-Uiracocha they assigned the chief power and command over all things; Montesinos that Illa-tici-Uiracocha was the name of the creator of the world; Molina that Tecsi-Uiracocha was the Creator and incomprehensible God; the anonymous Jesuit that Uiracocha meant the great God of "Pirua"; Betanzos that the Creator was Con-Tici-Uiracocha.

According to Montesinos and the anonymous Jesuit Uira or Vira is a corruption of Pirua meaning a depository. The first meaning of Cocha is a lake, but here it is held to signify profundity, abyss, space. The "Dweller in Space." Ticci or Tici is base or foundation, hence the founder. Illa means light. The anonymous Jesuit gives the meaning "Eternal Light" to Illa-Ticci. The word Con, given by Betanzos and Garcia, has no known meaning.

Pachacamac and Pachayachachi are attributes of the deity. Pacha means time or place, also the universe. Camac is the Ruler, Yachachi the Teacher. "The Ruler and Teacher of the Universe." The meaning and significance of the word Uiracocha has been very fully discussed by Señor

Don Leonardo Villar of Cuzco in a paper entitled Lexicologia Keshua Uiracocha (Lima, 1887).]
And when he had created the world he formed a race of giants of disproportioned greatness painted and sculptured, to see whether it would be well to make real men of that size. He then created men in his likeness as they are now; and they lived in darkness.

Viracocha ordered these people that they should live without quarrelling, and that they should know and serve him. He gave them a certain precept which they were to observe on pain of being confounded if they should break it. They kept this precept for some time, but it is not mentioned what it was. But as there arose among them the vices of pride and covetousness, they transgressed the precept of Viracocha Pachayachachi and falling, through this sin, under his indignation, he confounded and cursed them. Then some were turned into stones, others into other things, some were swallowed up by the earth, others by the sea, and over all there came a general flood which they call uñu pachacuti, which means "water that overturns the land." They say that it rained 60 days and nights, that it drowned all created things, and that there alone remained some vestiges of those who were turned into stones, as a memorial of the event, and as an example to posterity, in the edifices of Pucara, which are 60 leagues from Cuzco.

Some of the nations, besides the Cuzcos, also say that a few were saved from this flood to leave descendants for a future age. Each nation has its special fable which is told by its people, of how their first ancestors were saved from the waters of the deluge. That the ideas they had in their blindness may be understood, I will insert only one, told by the nation of the Cañaris, a land of Quito and Tumibamba, 400 leagues from Cuzco and more.

They say that in the time of the deluge called uñu pachacuti there was a mountain named Guasano in the province of Quito and near a town called Tumipampa. The natives still point it out. Up this mountain went two of the Cañaris named Ataorupagui and Cusicayo. As the waters increased the mountain kept rising and keeping above them in such a way that it was never covered by the waters of the flood. In this way the two Cañaris escaped. These two, who were brothers, when the waters abated after the flood, began to sow. One day when they had been at work, on returning to their hut, they found in it some small loaves of bread, and a jar of chicha, which is the beverage used in this country in place of wine, made of boiled maize. They did not know who had brought it, but they gave thanks to the Creator, eating and drinking of that provision. Next day the same thing happened. As they marvelled at this mystery, they were anxious to find out who brought the meals. So one day they hid themselves, to spy out the bringers of their food. While they were watching they saw two Cañari women preparing the victuals and putting them in the accustomed place. When about to depart the men tried to seize them, but they evaded their would-be captors and escaped. The Cañaris, seeing the mistake they had made in molesting those who had done them so much good, became sad and prayed to Viracocha for pardon for their sins, entreating him to let the women come back and give them the accustomed meals. The Creator granted their petition. The women came back and said to the Cañaris—"The Creator has thought it well that we should return to you, lest you should die of hunger." They brought them food. Then there was friendship between the women and the Cañari brothers, and one of the Cañari brothers had connexion with one of the women. Then, as the elder brother was drowned in a lake which was near, the survivor married one of the women, and had the other as a concubine. By them he had ten sons who formed two lineages of five each, and increasing in numbers they called one Hanansaya which is the same as to say the upper party, and the other Hurinsaya, or the lower party. From these all the Cañaris that now exist are descended[27].

[Note 27: The same story of the origin of the Cañaris is told by Molina, p. 8. But the mountain is called Huaca-yuan; and instead of women the beings who brought the food were macaws. Molina tells another story received from the people of Ancas-mayu. Both seem to have been obtained by asking leading questions about a deluge.]

In the same way the other nations have fables of how some of their people were saved from whom they trace their origin and descent. But the Incas and most of those of Cuzco, those among them who are believed to know most, do not say that anyone escaped from the flood, but that Viracocha began to create men afresh, as will be related further on. One thing is believed among all the nations of these parts, for they all speak generally and as well known of the general flood which they call uñu pachacuti. From this we may clearly understand that if, in these parts they have a tradition of the great flood, this great mass of the floating islands which they afterwards called the Atlanticas, and now the Indies of Castille or America must have begun to receive a population immediately after the flood, although, by their account, the details are different from those which the true Scriptures teach us. This must have been done by divine Providence, through the first people coming over the land of the Atlantic Island, which was joined to this, as has been already said. For as the natives, though barbarous, give reasons for their very ancient settlement, by recording the flood, there is no necessity for setting aside the Scriptures by quoting authorities to establish this origin. We now come to those who relate the events of the second age after the flood, which is the subject of the next chapter.

VII.FABLE OF THE SECOND AGE, AND CREATION OF THE BARBAROUS INDIANS ACCORDING TO THEIR ACCOUNT.

It is related that everything was destroyed in the flood called uñu pachacuti[28]. It must now be known that Viracocha Pachayachachi, when he destroyed that land as has been already recounted, preserved three men, one of them named Taguapaca, that they might serve and help him in the creation of new people who had to be made in the second age after the deluge, which was done in this manner. The flood being passed and the land dry, Viracocha determined to people it a second time, and, to make it more perfect, he decided upon creating luminaries to give it light. With this object he went, with his servants, to a great lake in the Collao, in which there is an island called Titicaca, the meaning being "the rock of lead," of which we shall treat in the first part. Viracocha went to this island, and presently ordered that the sun, moon, and stars should come forth, and be set in the heavens to give light to the world, and it was so. They say that the moon was created brighter than the sun, which made the sun jealous at the time when they rose into the sky. So the sun threw over the moon's face a handful of ashes, which gave it the shaded colour it now presents. This frontier lake of Chucuito, in the territory of the Collao, is 57 leagues to the south of Cuzco. Viracocha gave various orders to his servants, but Taguapaca disobeyed the commands of Viracocha. So Viracocha was enraged against Taguapaca, and ordered the other two servants to take him, tie him hands and feet, and launch him in a balsa on the lake. This was done. Taguapaca was blaspheming against Viracocha for the way he was treated, and threatening that he would return and take vengeance, when he was carried by the water down the drain of the same lake, and was not seen again for a long time. This done, Viracocha made a sacred idol in that place, as a place for worship and as a sign of what he had there created[29].

[Note 28: Uñu pachacuti would mean the world (pacha) overturned (cuti) by water (uñu). Probably a word coined by the priests, after putting leading questions about a universal deluge.]

[Note 29: This servant of Uiracocha is also mentioned by Cieza de Leon and Yamqui Pachacuti. Cieza appears to consider that Tuapaca was merely the name of Uiracocha in the Collao. Yamqui Pachacuti gives the names Tarapaca and Tonapa and connects them with Uiracocha. But he also uses the word Pachacca, a servant. These names are clearly the same as the Tahuapaca of Sarmiento. Tahua means four, but Sarmiento gives three as the number of these servants of Uiracocha. The meaning of paca is anything secret or mysterious, from pacani to hide. The names represent an ancient myth of some kind, but it is not possible, at this distance of time, to ascertain more than the names. Tonapa looks like a slip of the pen, and is probably Tarapa for Tarapaca. Don Samuel A. Lapone Quevedo published a mythological essay entitled El Culto de Tonapa with reference to the notice in the work of Yamqui Pachacuti; but he is given to speculations about phallic and solar worship, and to the arbitrary alteration of letters to fit into his theories.]

Leaving the island, he passed by the lake to the main land, taking with him the two servants who survived. He went to a place now called Tiahuanacu in the province of Colla-suyu, and in this place he sculptured and designed on a great piece of stone, all the nations that he intended to create. This done, he ordered his two servants to charge their memories with the names of all tribes that he had depicted, and of the valleys and provinces where they were to come forth, which were those of the whole land. He ordered that each one should go by a different road, naming the tribes, and ordering them all to go forth and people the country. His servants, obeying the command of Viracocha, set out on their journey and work. One went by the mountain range or chain which they call the heights over the plains on the South Sea. The other went by the heights which overlook the wonderful mountain ranges which we call the Andes, situated to the east of the said sea. By these roads they went, saying with a loud voice "Oh you tribes and nations, hear and obey the order of Ticci Viracocha Pachayachachi, which commands you to go forth, and multiply and settle the land." Viracocha himself did the same along the road between those taken by his two servants, naming all the tribes and places by which he passed. At the sound of his voice every place obeyed, and people came forth, some from lakes, others from fountains, valleys, caves, trees, rocks and hills, spreading over the land and multiplying to form the nations which are to-day in Peru.

Others affirm that this creation of Viracocha was made from the Titicaca site where, having originally formed some shapes of large strong men[30] which seemed to him out of proportion, he made them again of his stature which was, as they say, the average height of men, and being made he gave them life. Thence they set out to people the land. As they spoke one language previous to starting, they built those edifices, the ruins of which may still be seen, before they set out. This was for the residence of Viracocha, their maker. After departing they varied their languages, noting the cries of wild beasts, insomuch that, coming across each other afterwards, those could not understand who had before been relations and neighbours.

[Note 30: Jayaneo. This was the name given to giants in the books of chivalry. See Don Quijote, i. cap. 5, p. 43.]

Whether it was in one way or the other, all agree that Viracocha was the creator of these people. They have the tradition that he was a man of medium height, white and dressed in a white robe like an alb secured round the waist, and that he carried a staff and a book in his hands.

Besides this they tell of a strange event; how that Viracocha, after he had created all people, went on his road and came to a place where many men of his creation had congregated. This place is now called Cacha. When Viracocha arrived there, the inhabitants were estranged owing to his dress and bearing. They murmured at it and proposed to kill him from a hill that was near. They took their weapons there, and gathered together with evil intentions against Viracocha. He, falling on his knees on some plain ground, with his hands clasped, fire from above came down upon those on the hill, and covered all the place, burning up the earth and stones like straw.

Those bad men were terrified at the fearful fire. They came down from the hill, and sought pardon from Viracocha for their sin. Viracocha was moved by compassion. He went to the flames and put them out with his staff. But the hill remained quite parched up, the stones being rendered so light by the burning that a very large stone which could not have been carried on a cart, could be raised easily by one man. This may be seen at this day, and it is a wonderful sight to behold this hill, which is a quarter of a league in extent, all burnt up. It is in the Collao[31].
[Note 31: Not in the Collaos but in the valley of the Vilcamayu.
Afterwards a very remarkable temple was built there, described by Squier.]
After this Viracocha continued his journey and arrived at a place called Urcos, 6 leagues to the south of Cuzco. Remaining there some days he was well served by the natives of that neighbourhood. At the time of his departure, he made them a celebrated huaca or statue, for them to offer gifts to and worship; to which statue the Incas, in after times, offered many rich gifts of gold and other metals, and above all a golden bench. When the Spaniards entered Cuzco they found it, and appropriated it to themselves. It was worth $17,000. The Marquis Don Francisco Pizarro took it himself, as the share of the General.
Returning to the subject of the fable, Viracocha continued his journey, working his miracles and instructing his created beings. In this way he reached the territory on the equinoctial line, where are now Puerto Viejo and Manta. Here he was joined by his servants. Intending to leave the land of Peru, he made a speech to those he had created, apprising them of the things that would happen. He told them that people would come, who would say that they were Viracocha their creator, and that they were not to believe them; but that in the time to come he would send his messengers who would protect and teach them. Having said this he went to sea with his two servants, and went travelling over the water as if it was land, without sinking. For they appeared like foam over the water and the people, therefore, gave them the name of Viracocha which is the same as to say the grease or foam of the sea[32]. At the end of some years after Viracocha departed, they say that Taguapaca, who Viracocha ordered to be thrown into the lake of Titicaca in the Collao, as has already been related, came back and began, with others, to preach that he was Viracocha. Although at first the people were doubtful, they finally saw that it was false, and ridiculed them[33].
[Note 32: A mistake. See Garcilasso de la Vega, ii. p. 66.]
[Note 33: This story is told in a somewhat different form by Yamqui Pachacuti, p. 72.]
This absurd fable of their creation is held by these barbarians and they affirm and believe it as if they had really seen it to happen and come to pass[34].
[Note 34: The tradition of the exercise of his creative powers by Viracocha at lake Titicaca, is derived from the more ancient people who were the builders of Tiahuanacu. Besides Sarmiento, the authors who give this Titicaca Myth are Garcilasso de la Vega, Cieza de Leon, Molina, Betanzos, Yamqui Pachacuti, Polo de Ondegardo, and the anonymous Jesuit. Acosta, Montesinos, Balboa and Santillana are silent respecting it.]

VIII. THE ANCIENT BEHETRIAS[35] OF THESE KINGDOMS OF PERU AND THEIR PROVINCES.

It is important to note that these barbarians could tell nothing more respecting what happened from the second creation by Viracocha down to the time of the Incas. But it may be assumed that, although the land was peopled and full of inhabitants before the Incas, it had no regular government, nor did it have natural lords elected by common consent to govern and rule, and who were respected by the people, so that they were obeyed and received tribute. On the contrary all the people were scattered and disorganized, living in complete liberty, and each man being sole lord of his house and estate. In each tribe there were two divisions. One was called Hanansaya, which means the upper division, and the other Hurinsaya, which is the lower division, a custom which continues to this day. These divisions do not mean anything more than a way to count each other, for their satisfaction, though afterwards it served a more useful purpose, as will be seen in its place.

[Note 35: Behetria. A condition of perfect equality without any distinction of rank. Freedom from the subjection of any lord.]

As there were dissensions among them, a certain kind of militia was organized for defence, in the following way. When it became known to the people of one district that some from other parts were coming to make war, they chose one who was a native, or he might be a stranger, who was known to be a valiant warrior. Often such a man offered himself to aid and to fight for them against their enemies. Such a man was followed and his orders were obeyed during the war. When the war was over he became a private man as he had been before, like the rest of the people, nor did they pay him tribute either before or afterwards, nor any manner of tax whatever. To such a man they gave and still give the name of Sinchi which means valiant. They call such men "Sinchi-cuna" which means "valiant now" as who should say—"now during the time the war lasts you shall be our valiant man, and afterwards no ": or another meaning would be simply "valiant men," for "cuna" is an adverb of time, and also denotes the plural[36]. In whichever meaning, it is very applicable to these temporary captains in the days of behetrias and general liberty. So that from the general flood of which they have a tradition to the time when the Incas began to reign, which was 3519 years, all the natives of these kingdoms lived on their properties without acknowledging either a natural or an elected lord. They succeeded in preserving, as it is said, a simple state of liberty, living in huts or caves or humble little houses. This name of "Sinchi" for those who held sway only during war, lasted throughout the land until the time of Tupac Inca Yupanqui, the tenth Inca, who instituted "Curacas" and other officials in the order which will be fully described in the life of that Inca. Even at the present time they continue this use and custom in the provinces of Chile and in other parts of the forests of Peru to the east of Quito and Chachapoyas, where they only obey a chief during war time, not any special one, but he who is known to be most valiant, enterprising and daring in the wars. The reader should note that all the land was private property with reference to any dominion of chiefs, yet they had natural chiefs with special rights in each province, as for instance among the natives of the valley of Cuzco and in other parts, as we shall relate of each part in its place.

[Note 36: Cinchicona. Sinchi means strong. Cuna is the plural particle. Sinchi was the name for a chief or leader. I have not met with cuna as an adverb of time and meaning "now." No such meaning is given in the Grammar of Domingo de Santo Tomas, which was published in 1560, twelve years before Sarmiento wrote.]

IX. THE FIRST SETTLERS IN THE VALLEY OF CUZCO.

I have explained how the people of these lands preserved their inheritances and lived on them in ancient times, and that their proper and natural countries were known. There were many of these which I shall notice in their places, treating specially at present of the original settlers of the valley where stands the present city of Cuzco. For from there we have to trace the origin of the tyranny of the Incas, who always had their chief seat in the valley of Cuzco.

Before all things it must be understood that the valley of Cuzco is in 130° 15' from the equator on the side of the south pole[37]. In this valley, owing to its being fertile for cultivation, there were three tribes settled from most ancient times, the first called Sauaseras, the second Antasayas, the third Huallas. They settled near each other, although their lands for sowing were distinct, which is the property they valued most in those days and even now. These natives of the valley lived there in peace for many years, cultivating their farms.

[Note 37: 13° 31'. He is 16 miles out in his latitude.]

Some time before the arrival of the Incas, three Sinchis, strangers to this valley, the first named Alcabisa[38], the second Copalimayta, and the third Culunchima, collected certain companies and came to the valley of Cuzco, where, by consent of the natives, they settled and became brothers and companions of the original inhabitants. So they lived for a long time. There was concord between these six tribes, three native and three immigrant. They relate that the immigrants came out to where the Incas then resided, as we shall relate presently, and called them relations. This is an important point with reference to what happened afterwards.

[Note 38: The Alcabisas, as original inhabitants of the Cuzco valley, are mentioned by Cieza de Leon (ii. p. 105) who calls them Alcaviquiza. Betanzos has Alcaviya, and Balboa Allcay-villcas. Cieza describes the victory over them by Mayta Ccapac. Yamqui Pachacuti gives Allcayviesas, Cullinchinas, and Cayancachis as the names of the tribes who originally inhabited the Cuzco valley. Cayancachi is a southern suburb of Cuzco outside the Huatanay river.]

Before entering upon the history of the Incas I wish to make known or, speaking more accurately, to answer a difficulty which may occur to those who have not been in these parts. Some may say that this history cannot be accepted as authentic being taken from the narratives of these barbarians, because, having no letters, they could not preserve such details as they give from so remote an antiquity. The answer is that, to supply the want of letters, these barbarians had a curious invention which was very good and accurate. This was that from one to the other, from fathers to sons, they handed down past events, repeating the story of them many times, just as lessons are repeated from a professor's chair, making the hearers say these historical lessons over and over again until they were fixed in the memory. Thus each one of the descendants continued to communicate the annals in the order described with a view to preserve their histories and deeds, their ancient traditions, the numbers of their tribes, towns, provinces, their days, months and years, their battles, deaths, destructions, fortresses and "Sinchis." Finally they recorded, and they still record, the most notable things which consist in their numbers (or statistics), on certain cords called quipu, which is the same as to say reasoner or accountant. On these cords they make certain knots by which, and by differences of colour, they distinguish and record each thing as by letters. It is a thing to be admired to see what details may be recorded on these cords, for which there are masters like our writing masters[39].

[Note 39: The system of recording by quipus is described by Garcilasso de la Vega, i. pp. 150 and 191, also ii. p. 117 and more fully at ii. pp. 121—125. Cieza de Leon mentions the quipu system in his first part (see i. p. 291 and note) and in the second part (ii. pp. 33—35, 53, 57, 61,165). At p. 32 the method of preserving the memory of former events is described very much as in the text. See also Molina, pp. 10, 169. Molina also describes the boards on which historical events were painted, p. 4. They were, he says, kept in a temple near Cuzco, called Poquen-cancha. See also Cieza de Leon (second part), p. 28.]

Besides this they had, and still have, special historians in these nations, an hereditary office descending from father to son. The collection of these annals is due to the great diligence of Pachacuti Inca Yupanqui, the ninth Inca, who sent out a general summons to all the old historians in all the provinces he had subjugated, and even to many others throughout those kingdoms. He had them in Cuzco for a long time, examining them concerning their antiquities, origin, and the most notable events in their history. These were painted on great boards, and deposited in the temple of the Sun, in a great hall. There such boards, adorned with gold, were kept as in our libraries, and learned persons were appointed, who were well versed in the art of understanding and declaring their contents. No one was allowed to enter where these boards were kept, except the Inca and the historians, without a special order of the Inca.

In this way they took care to have all their past history investigated, and to have records respecting all kinds of people, so that at this day the Indians generally know and agree respecting details and important events, though, in some things, they hold different opinions on special points. By examining the oldest and most prudent among them, in all ranks of life, who had most credit, I collected and compiled the present history, referring the sayings and declarations of one party to their antagonists of another party, for they are divided into parties, and seeking from each one a memorial of its lineage and of that of the opposing party. These memorials, which are all in my possession, were compared and corrected, and ultimately verified in public, in presence of representatives of all the parties and lineages, under oaths in presence of a judge, and with expert and very faithful interpreters also on oath, and I thus finished what is now written. Such great diligence has been observed, because a thing which is the foundation of the true completion of such a great work as the establishment of the tyranny of the cruel Incas of this land will make all the nations of the world understand the judicial and more than legitimate right that the King of Castille has to these Indies and to other lands adjacent, especially to these kingdoms of Peru. As all the histories of past events have been verified by proof, which in this case has been done so carefully and faithfully by order and owing to the industry of the most excellent Viceroy Don Francisco de Toledo, no one can doubt that everything in this volume is most sufficiently established and verified without any room being left for reply or contradiction. I have been desirous of making this digression because, in writing the history, I have heard that many entertain the doubts I have above referred to, and it seemed well to satisfy them once for all.

X.HOW THE INCAS BEGAN TO TYRANNIZE OVER THE LANDS AND INHERITANCES.

Having explained that, in ancient times, all this land was owned by the people, it is necessary to state how the Incas began their tyranny. Although the tribes all lived in simple liberty without recognising any lord, there were always some ambitious men among them, aspiring for mastery. They committed violence among their countrymen and among strangers to subject them and bring them to obedience under their command, so that they might serve them and pay tribute. Thus bands of men belonging to one region went to others to make war and to rob and kill, usurping the lands of others.

As these movements took place in many parts by many tribes, each one trying to subjugate his neighbour, it happened that 6 leagues from the valley of Cuzco, at a place called Paccari-tampu, there were four men with their four sisters, of fierce courage and evil intentions, although with lofty aims. These, being more able than the others, understood the pusillanimity of the natives of those districts and the ease with which they could be made to believe anything that was propounded with authority or with any force. So they conceived among themselves the idea of being able to subjugate many lands by force and deception. Thus all the eight brethren, four men and four women, consulted together how they could tyrannize over other tribes beyond the place where they lived, and they proposed to do this by violence. Considering that most of the natives were ignorant and could easily be made to believe what was said to them, particularly if they were addressed with some roughness, rigour and authority, against which they could make neither reply nor resistance, because they are timid by nature, they sent abroad certain fables respecting their origin, that they might be respected and feared. They said that they were the sons of Viracocha Pachayachachi, the Creator, and that they had come forth out of certain windows to rule the rest of the people. As they were fierce, they made the people believe and fear them, and hold them to be more than men, even worshipping them as gods. Thus they introduced the religion that suited them. The order of the fable they told of their origin was as follows.

XI. THE FABLE OF THE ORIGIN OF THE INCAS OF CUZCO.

All the native Indians of this land relate and affirm that the Incas Ccapac originated in this way. Six leagues S.S.W. of Cuzco by the road which the Incas made, there is a place called Paccari-tampu, which means "the house of production[40]" at which there is a hill called Tampu-tocco, meaning "the house of windows." It is certain that in this hill there are three windows, one called "Maras-tocco," the other "Sutic-tocco," while that which is in the middle, between these two, was known as "Ccapac-tocco," which means "the rich window," because they say that it was ornamented with gold and other treasures. From the window called "Maras-tocco" came forth, without parentage, a tribe of Indians called Maras. There are still some of them in Cuzco. From the "Sutic-tocco" came Indians called Tampus, who settled round the same hill, and there are also men of this lineage still in Cuzco. From the chief window of "Ccapac-tocco," came four men and four women, called brethren. These knew no father nor mother, beyond the story they told that they were created and came out of the said window by order of Ticci Viracocha, and they declared that Viracocha created them to be lords. For this reason they took the name of Inca, which is the same as lord. They took "Ccapac" as an additional name because they came out of the window "Ccapac-tocco," which means "rich," although afterwards they used this term to denote the chief lord over many.

[Note 40: Correctly "the tavern of the dawn."]

The names of the eight brethren were as follows: The eldest of the men, and the one with the most authority was named MANCO CCAPAC, the second AYAR AUCA, the third AYAR CACHI, the fourth AYAR UCHU. Of the women the eldest was called MAMA OCCLO, the second MAMA HUACO, the third MAMA IPACURA, or, as others say, MAMA CURA, the fourth MAMA RAUA.

The eight brethren, called Incas, said—"We are born strong and wise, and with the people who will here join us, we shall be powerful. We will go forth from this place to seek fertile lands and when we find them we will subjugate the people and take the lands, making war on all those who do not receive us as their lords," This, as they relate, was said by Mama Huaco, one of the women, who was fierce and cruel. Manco Ccapac, her brother, was also cruel and atrocious. This being agreed upon between the eight, they began to move the people who lived near the hill, putting it to them that their reward would be to become rich and to receive the lands and estates of those who were conquered and subjugated. For these objects they moved ten tribes or ayllus, which means among these barbarians "lineages" or "parties"; the names of which are as follows:

I. CHAUIN CUZCO AYLLU of the lineage of AYAR CACHI, of which there are still some in Cuzco, the chiefs being MARTIN CHUCUMBI, and DON DIEGO HUAMAN PAOCAR.

II. ARAYRACA AYLLU CUZCO-CALLAN. At present there are of this ayllu JUAN PIZARRO YUPANQUI, DON FRANCISCO QUISPI, ALONSO TARMA YUPANQUI of the lineage of AYAR UCHU.

III. TARPUNTAY AYLLU. Of this there are now some in Cuzco.
IV. HUACAYTAQUI AYLLU. Some still living in Cuzco.
V. SAÑOC AYLLU. Some still in Cuzco.
The above five lineages are HANAN-CUZCO, which means the party of Upper Cuzco.
VI. SUTIC-TOCCO AYLLU is the lineage which came out of one of the windows called "SUTIC-TOCCO," as has been before explained. Of these there are still some in Cuzco, the chiefs being DON FRANCISCO AVCA MICHO AVRI SUTIC, and DON ALONSO HUALPA.
VII. MARAS AYLLU. These are of the men who came forth from the window "MARAS-TOCCO." There are some of these now in Cuzco, the chiefs being DON ALONSO LLAMA OCA, and DON GONZALO AMPURA LLAMA OCA.
VIII. CUYCUSA AYLLU. Of these there are still some in Cuzco, the chief being CRISTOVAL ACLLARI.
IX. MASCA AYLLU. Of this there is in Cuzco—JUAN QUISPI.
X. ORO AYLLU. Of this lineage is DON PEDRO YUCAY.
I say that all these ayllus have preserved their records in such a way that the memory of them has not been lost. There are more of them than are given above, for I only insert the chiefs who are the protectors and heads of the lineages, under whose guidance they are preserved. Each chief has the duty and obligation to protect the rest, and to know the history of his ancestors. Although I say that these live in Cuzco, the truth is that they are in a suburb of the city which the Indians call Cayocache and which is known to us as Belem, from the church of that parish which is that of our Lady of Belem.
Returning to our subject, all these followers above mentioned marched with Manco Ccapac and the other brethren to seek for land [and to tyrannize over those who did no harm to them, nor gave them any excuse for war, and without any right or title beyond what has been stated]. To be prepared for war they chose for their leaders Manco Ccapac and Mama Huaco, and with this arrangement the companies of the hill of Tampu-tocco set out, to put their design into execution.

XII.THE ROAD WHICH THESE COMPANIES OF THE INCAS TOOK TO THE VALLEY OF CUZCO, AND OF THE FABLES WHICH ARE MIXED WITH THEIR HISTORY.

The Incas and the rest of the companies or ayllus set out from their homes at Tampu-tocco, taking with them their property and arms, in sufficient numbers to form a good squadron, having for their chiefs the said Manco Ccapac and Mama Huaco. Manco Ccapac took with him a bird like a falcon, called indi[41], which they all worshipped and feared as a sacred, or, as some say, an enchanted thing, for they thought that this bird made Manco Ccapac their lord and obliged the people to follow him. It was thus that Manco Ccapac gave them to understand, and it was carried in vahidos[42], always kept in a covered hamper of straw, like a box, with much care. He left it as an heirloom to his son, and the Incas had it down to the time of Inca Yupanqui. In his hand he carried with him a staff of gold, to test the lands which they would come to.
[Note 41: This bird called indi, the familiar spirit of Manco Ccapac, is not mentioned by any other author. There is more about it in the life of Mayta Ccapac, the great-grandson of Manco Ccapac. The word seems to be the same as Ynti the Sun-God.]
[Note 42: Vahido means giddiness, vertigo.]
Marching together they came to a place called Huana-cancha, four leagues from the valley of

Cuzco, where they remained for some time, sowing and seeking for fertile land. Here Manco Ccapac had connexion with his sister Mama Occlo, and she became pregnant by him. As this place did not appear able to sustain them, being barren, they advanced to another place called Tampu-quiro, where Mama Occlo begot a son named Sinchi Rocca. Having celebrated the natal feasts of the infant, they set out in search of fertile land, and came to another place called Pallata, which is almost contiguous to Tampu-quiro, and there they remained for some years.

Not content with this land, they came to another called Hays-quisro, a quarter of a league further on. Here they consulted together over what ought to be done respecting their journey, and over the best way of getting rid of Ayar Cachi, one of the four brothers. Ayar Cachi was fierce and strong, and very dexterous with the sling. He committed great cruelties and was oppressive both among the natives of the places they passed, and among his own people. The other brothers were afraid that the conduct of Ayar Cachi would cause their companies to disband and desert, and that they would be left alone. As Manco Ccapac was prudent, he concurred with the opinion of the others that they should secure their object by deceit. They called Ayar Cachi and said to him, "Brother! Know that in Ccapac-tocco we have forgotten the golden vases called tupac-cusi[43], and certain seeds, and the napa[44], which is our principal ensign of sovereignty." The napa is a sheep of the country, the colour white, with a red body cloth, on the top ear-rings of gold, and on the breast a plate with red badges such as was worn by rich Incas when they went abroad; carried in front of all on a pole with a cross of plumes of feathers. This was called suntur-paucar[45]. They said that it would be for the good of all, if he would go back and fetch them. When Ayar Cachi refused to return, his sister Mama Huaco, raising her foot, rebuked him with furious words, saying, "How is it that there should be such cowardice in so strong a youth as you are? Get ready for the journey, and do not fail to go to Tampu-tocco, and do what you are ordered." Ayar Cachi was shamed by these words. He obeyed and started to carry out his orders. They gave him, as a companion, one of those who had come with them, named Tampu-chacay, to whom they gave secret orders to kill Ayar Cachi at Tampu-tocco, and not to return with him. With these orders they both arrived at Tampu-tocco. They had scarcely arrived when Ayar Cachi entered through the window Ccapac-tocco, to get the things for which he had been sent. He was no sooner inside than Tampu-chacay, with great celerity, put a rock against the opening of the window and sat upon it, that Ayar Cachi might remain inside and die there. When Ayar Cachi turned to the opening and found it closed he understood the treason of which the traitor Tampu-chacay had been guilty, and determined to get out if it was possible, to take vengeance. To force an opening he used such force and shouted so loud that he made the mountain tremble. With a loud voice he spoke these words to Tampu-chacay, "Thou traitor! thou who hast done me so much harm, thinkest thou to convey the news of my mortal imprisonment? That shall never happen. For thy treason thou shalt remain outside, turned into a stone." So it was done, and to this day they show the stone on one side of the window Ccapac-tocco. Turn we now to the seven brethren who had remained at Hays-quisro. The death of Ayar Cachi being known, they were very sorry for what they had done, for, as he was valiant, they regretted much to be without him when the time came to make war on any one. So they mourned for him. This Ayar Cachi was so dexterous with a sling and so strong that with each shot he pulled down a mountain and filled up a ravine. They say that the ravines, which we now see on their line of march, were made by Ayar Cachi in hurling stones.

[Note 43: Tupac-cusi, meaning golden vases, does not occur elsewhere. It may be a mis-print for tupac-ccuri, tupac meaning anything royal and ccuri gold.]

[Note 44: Napa was the name of a sacred figure of a llama, one of the insignia of royalty. See

Molina, pp. 19, 39, 47. The verb napani is to salute, napay, salutation. Raymi-napa was the flock dedicated for sacrifice.]

[Note 45: Suntur-paucar was the head-dress of the Inca. See Balboa, p. 20. Literally the "brilliant circle." See also Molina, pp. 6, 17, 39, 42, 44, and Yamqui Pachacuti, pp. 14, 106, 120.]

The seven Incas and their companions left this place, and came to another called Quirirmanta at the foot of a hill which was afterwards called Huanacauri. In this place they consulted together how they should divide the duties of the enterprise amongst themselves, so that there should be distinctions between them. They agreed that as Manco Ccapac had had a child by his sister, they should be married and have children to continue the lineage, and that he should be the leader. Ayar Uchu was to remain as a huaca for the sake of religion. Ayar Auca, from the position they should select, was to take possession of the land set apart for him to people.

Leaving this place they came to a hill at a distance of two leagues, a little more or less, from Cuzco. Ascending the hill they saw a rainbow, which the natives call huanacauri. Holding it to be a fortunate sign, Manco Ccapac said: "Take this for a sign that the world will not be destroyed by water. We shall arrive and from hence we shall select where we shall found our city." Then, first casting lots, they saw that the signs were good for doing so, and for exploring the land from that point and becoming lords of it. Before they got to the height where the rainbow was, they saw a huaca which was a place of worship in human shape, near the rainbow. They determined among themselves to seize it and take it away from there. Ayar Uchu offered himself to go to it, for they said that he was very like it. When Ayar Uchu came to the statue or huaca, with great courage he sat upon it, asking it what it did there. At these words the huaca turned its head to see who spoke, but, owing to the weight upon it, it could not see. Presently, when Ayar Uchu wanted to get off he was not able, for he found that the soles of his feet were fastened to the shoulders of the huaca. The six brethren, seeing that he was a prisoner, came to succour him. But Ayar Uchu, finding himself thus transformed, and that his brethren could not release him, said to them—"O Brothers, an evil work you have wrought for me. It was for your sakes that I came where I must remain for ever, apart from your company. Go! go! happy brethren, I announce to you that you will be great lords. I, therefore, pray that in recognition of the desire I have always had to please you, you will honour and venerate me in all your festivals and ceremonies, and that I shall be the first to whom you make offerings. For I remain here for your sakes. When you celebrate the huarachico (which is the arming of the sons as knights) you shall adore me as their father, for I shall remain here for ever." Manco Ccapac answered that he would do so, for that it was his will and that it should be so ordered. Ayar Uchu promised for the youths that he would bestow on them the gifts of valour, nobility, and knighthood, and with these last words he remained, turned into stone. They constituted him the huaca of the Incas, giving it the name of Ayar Uchu Huanacauri.[46] And so it always was, until the arrival of the Spaniards, the most venerated huaca, and the one that received the most offerings of any in the kingdom. Here the Incas went to arm the young knights until about twenty years ago, when the Christians abolished this ceremony. It was religiously done, because there were many abuses and idolatrous practices, offensive and contrary to the ordinances of God our Lord.

[Note 46: Huanacauri was a very sacred huaca of the Peruvians. Cieza de Leon tells much the same story as Sarmiento, ii. pp. 17, 18, 19, 22, 89, 101, 107, 111. Garcilasso de la Vega mentions Huanacauri four times, i. pp. 65, 66, and ii. pp. 169, 230, as a place held in great veneration. It is frequently mentioned by Molina. The word is given by Yamqui Pachacuti as Huayna-captiy. Huayna means a youth, captiy is the subjunctive of the verb cani, I am. The word appears to have reference to the arming of youths, and the ordeals they went through, which took place annually

XIII.ENTRY OF THE INCAS INTO THE VALLEY OF CUZCO, AND THE FABLES THEY RELATE CONCERNING IT.

The six brethren were sad at the loss of Ayar Uchu, and at the loss of Ayar Cachi; and, owing to the death of Ayar Cachi, those of the lineage of the Incas, from that time to this day, always fear to go to Tampu-tocco, lest they should have to remain there like Ayar Cachi.

They went down to the foot of the hill, whence they began their entry into the valley of Cuzco, arriving at a place called Matahua, where they stopped and built huts, intending to remain there some time. Here they armed as knight the son of Manco Ccapac and of Mama Occlo, named Sinchi Rocca, and they bored his ears, a ceremony which is called huarachico, being the insignia of his knighthood and nobility, like the custom known among ourselves. On this occasion they indulged in great rejoicings, drinking for many days, and at intervals mourning for the loss of their brother Ayar Uchu. It was here that they invented the mourning sound for the dead, like the cooing of a dove. Then they performed the dance called Ccapac Raymi, a ceremony of the royal or great lords. It is danced, in long purple robes, at the ceremonies they call quicochico[47], which is when girls come to maturity, and the huarachico[48], when they bore the ears of the Incas, and the rutuchico[49] when the Inca's hair is cut the first time, and the ayuscay[50], which is when a child is born, and they drink continuously for four or five days.

[Note 47: Quicu-chicuy was the ceremony when girls attained puberty. The customs, on this occasion, are described by Molina, p. 53. See also Yamqui Pachacuti, p. 80, and the anonymous Jesuit, p. 181.]

[Note 48: Huarachicu was the great festival when the youths went through their ordeals, and were admitted to manhood and to bear arms. Garcilasso de la Vega gives the word as "Huaracu"; and fully describes the ordeals and the ceremonies, ii. pp. 161—178. See also Molina, pp. 34 and 41—46, and Yamqui Pachacuti, p. 80.]

[Note 49: Rutuchicu is the ceremony when a child reaches the age of one year, from rutuni, to cut or shear. It receives the name which it retains until the Huarachicu if a boy, and until the Quicu-chicuy if a girl. They then receive the names they retain until death. At the Rutuchicu the child was shorn. Molina, p. 53.]

[Note 50: Molina says that Ayuscay was the ceremony when the woman conceives. Molina, p. 53.]

After this they were in Matahua for two years, waiting to pass on to the upper valley to seek good and fertile land. Mama Huaco, who was very strong and dexterous, took two wands of gold and hurled them towards the north. One fell, at two shots of an arquebus, into a ploughed field called Colcapampa and did not drive in well, the soil being loose and not terraced. By this they knew that the soil was not fertile. The other went further, to near Cuzco, and fixed well in the territory called Huanay-pata, where they knew the land to be fertile. Others say that this proof was made by Manco Ccapac with the staff of gold which he carried himself, and that thus they knew of the fertility of the land, when the staff sunk in the land called Huanay-pata, two shots of an arquebus from Cuzco. They knew the crust of the soil to be rich and close, so that it could only be broken by using much force.

Let it be by one way or the other, for all agree that they went trying the land with a pole or staff until they arrived at this Huanay-pata, when they were satisfied. They were sure of its fertility, because after sowing perpetually, it always yielded abundantly, giving more the more it was sown. They determined to usurp that land by force, in spite of the natural owners, and to do with it as they chose. So they returned to Matahua.

From that place Manco Ccapac saw a heap of stones near the site of the present monastery of Santo Domingo at Cuzco. Pointing it out to his brother Ayar Auca, he said, "Brother! you remember how it was arranged between us, that you should go to take possession of the land where we are to settle. Well! look at that stone." Pointing out the stone he continued, "Go thither flying," for they say that Ayar Auca had developed some wings, "and seating yourself there, take possession of land seen from that heap of stones. We will presently come to settle and reside." When Ayar Auca heard the words of his brother, he opened his wings and flew to that place which Manco Ccapac had pointed out. Seating himself there, he was presently turned into stone, and was made the stone of possession. In the ancient language of this valley the heap was called cozco, whence that site has had the name of Cuzco to this day[51]. From this circumstance the Incas had a proverb which said, "Ayar Auca cuzco huanca," or, "Ayar Auca a heap of marble." Others say that Manco Ccapac gave the name of Cuzco because he wept in that place where he buried his brother Ayar Cachi. Owing to his sorrow and to the fertility he gave that name which in the ancient language of that time signified sad as well as fertile. The first version must be the correct one because Ayar Cachi was not buried at Cuzco, having died at Ccapac-tocco as has been narrated before. And this is generally affirmed by Incas and natives.

[Note 51: Cuzco means a clod, or hard unirrigated land. Cuzquini is to break clods of earth, or to level. Montesinos derives the name of the city from the verb "to level," or from the heaps of clods, of earth called cuzco. Cusquic-Raymi is the month of June.]

Five brethren only remaining, namely Manco Ccapac, and the four sisters, and Manco Ccapac being the only surviving brother out of four, they presently resolved to advance to where Ayar Auca had taken possession. Manco Ccapac first gave to his son Sinchi Rocca a wife named Mama Cuca, of the lineage of Sañu, daughter of a Sinchi named Sitic-huaman, by whom he afterwards had a son named Sapaca. He also instituted the sacrifice called capa cocha[52], which is the immolation of two male and two female infants before the idol Huanacauri, at the time when the Incas were armed as knights. These things being arranged, he ordered the companies to follow him to the place where Ayar Auca was.

[Note 52: Ccapac-cocha. The weight of evidence is, on the whole, in favour of this sacrifice of two infants having taken place at the Huarachicu, Cieza de Leon, in remarking that the Spaniards falsely imputed crimes to the Indians to justify their ill-treatment, says that the practice of human sacrifice was exaggerated, ii. pp. 79, 80. See also Molina, pp-54, 57. Yamqui Pachacuti, p. 86.]

Arriving on the land of Huanay-pata, which is near where now stands the Arco de la plata leading to the Charcas road, he found settled there a nation of Indians named Huallas, already mentioned. Manco Ccapac and Mama Occlo began to settle and to take possession of the land and water, against the will of the Huallas. On this business they did many violent and unjust things. As the Huallas attempted to defend their lives and properties, many cruelties were committed by Manco Ccapac and Mama Occlo. They relate that Mama Occlo was so fierce that, having killed one of the Hualla Indians, she cut him up, took out the inside, carried the heart and lungs in her mouth, and with an ayuinto, which is a stone fastened to a rope, in her hand, she attacked the Huallas with diabolical resolution. When the Huallas beheld this horrible and inhuman spectacle, they feared that the same thing would be done to them, being simple and timid, and they fled and abandoned their rights. Mama Occlo reflecting on her cruelty, and fearing that for it they would be branded as tyrants, resolved not to spare any Huallas, believing that the affair would thus be forgotten. So they killed all they could lay their hands upon, dragging infants from their mothers' wombs, that no memory might be left of these miserable Huallas.

Having done this Manco Ccapac advanced, and came within a mile of Cuzco to the S.E., where a Sinchi named Copalimayta came out to oppose him. We have mentioned this chief before and that, although he was a late comer, he settled with the consent of the natives of the valley, and had been incorporated in the nation of Sauaseray Panaca, natives of the site of Santo Domingo at Cuzco. Having seen the strangers invading their lands and tyrannizing over them, and knowing the cruelties inflicted on the Huallas, they had chosen Copalimayta as their Sinchi. He came forth to resist the invasion, saying that the strangers should not enter his lands or those of the natives. His resistance was such that Manco Ccapac and his companions were obliged to turn their backs. They returned to Huanay-pata, the land they had usurped from the Huallas. From the sowing they had made they derived a fine crop of maize, and for this reason they gave the place a name which means something precious[53].

[Note 53: The origin of the Inca dynasty derived from Manco Ccapac and his brethren issuing from the window at Paccari-tampu may be called the Paccari-tampu myth. It was universally received and believed. Garcilasso de la Vega gives the meanings of the names of the brothers. Ayar Cachi means salt or instruction in rational life, Ayar Uchu is pepper, meaning the delight experienced from such teaching, and Ayar Sauca means pleasure, or the joy they afterwards experienced from it. Balboa gives an account of the death of Ayar Cachi, but calls him Ayar Auca. He also describes the turning into stone at Huanacauri. Betanzos tells much the same story as Sarmiento; as do Cieza de Leon and Montesinos, with some slight differences. Yamqui Pachacuti gives the names of the brothers, but only relates the Huanacauri part of the story. Montesinos and Garcilasso de la Vega call one of the brothers Ayar Sauca. Sarmiento, Betanzos and Balboa call him Ayar Auca. All agree in the names of the other brothers.]

After some months they returned to the attack on the natives of the valley, to tyrannize over them. They assaulted the settlement of the Sauaseras, and were so rapid in their attack that they captured Copalimayta, slaughtering many of the Sauaseras with great cruelty. Copalimayta, finding himself a prisoner and fearing death, fled out of desperation, leaving his estates, and was never seen again after he escaped. Mama Huaco and Manco Ccapac usurped his houses, lands and people. In this way MANCO CCAPAC, MAMA HUACO, SINCHI ROCCA, and MANCO SAPACA settled on the site between the two rivers, and erected the House of the Sun, which they called YNTI-CANCHA. They divided all that position, from Santo Domingo to the junction of the rivers into four neighbourhoods or quarters which they call cancha. They called one QUINTI-CANCHA, the second CHUMPI-CANCHA, the third SAYRI-CANCHA, and the fourth YARAMPUY-CANCHA. They divided the sites among themselves, and thus the city was peopled, and, from the heap of stones of Ayar Auca it was called CUZCO[54].

[Note 54: Garcilasso de la Vega gives the most detailed description of the city of Cuzco and its suburbs, ii. p. 235, but he does not mention these four divisions. The space from Santo Domingo to the junction of the rivers only covers a few acres; and was devoted to the gardens of the Sun.]

XIV.THE DIFFERENCE BETWEEN MANCO CCAPAC AND THE ALCABISAS, RESPECTING THE ARABLE LAND.

It has been said that one of the natural tribes of this valley of Cuzco was the Alcabisas. At the time when Manco Ccapac settled at Ynti-cancha and seized the goods of the Sauaseras and Huallas, the Alcabisas were settled half an arquebus shot from Ynti-canchi, towards the part where Santa Clara now stands. Manco Ccapac had a plan to spread out his forces that his tyrannical intentions might not be impeded, so he sent his people, as if loosely and idly, making free with the land. He took the lands without distinction, to support his companies. As he had taken those of the Huallas and Sauaseras, he wished also to take those of the Alcabisas. As these Alcabisas had given up some, Manco Ccapac wished and intended to take all or nearly all. When the Alcabisas saw that the new comers even entered their houses, they said: "These are men who are bellicose and unreasonable! they take our lands! Let us set up landmarks on the fields they have left to us." This they did, but Mama Huaco said to Manco Ccapac, "let us take all the water from the Alcabisas, and then they will be obliged to give us the rest of their land." This was done and they took away the water. Over this there were disputes; but as the followers of Manco Ccapac were more and more masterful, they forced the Alcabisas to give up their lands which they wanted, and to serve them as their lords, although the Alcabisas never voluntarily served Manco Ccapac nor looked upon him as their lord. On the contrary they always went about saying with loud voices-to those of Manco Ccapac—"Away! away! out of our territory." For this Manco Ccapac was more hard upon them, and oppressed them tyrannically.

Besides the Alcabisas there were other tribes, as we have mentioned before. These Manco Ccapac and Mama Huaco totally destroyed, and more especially one which lived near Ynti-cancha, in the nearest land, called Humanamean, between Ynti-cancha and Cayocachi[55], where there also lived another native Sinchi named Culunchima. Manco Ccapac entered the houses and lands of all the natives, especially of the Alcabisas, condemned their Sinchi to perpetual imprisonment, sending the others to banishment in Cayocachi, and forcing them to pay tribute. But they were always trying to free themselves from the tyranny, as the Alcabisas did later[56].

[Note 55: Garcilasso de la Vega describes Cayau-cachi as a small village of about 300 inhabitants in his time. It was about 1000 paces west of the nearest house of the city in 1560; but he had been told that, at the time of his writing in 1602, the houses had been extended so as to include it.]

[Note 56: Cieza de Leon and Balboa corroborate the story of Sarmiento that the Alcabisas (Cieza calls them Alcaviquizas, Balboa has Allcay-villcas) were hostile to the Incas, Cieza, ii. p. 105, Balboa, p. 25. Yamqui Pachacuti mentions them as Allcayviesas, p. 76.]

Having completed the yoke over the natives, their goods and persons, Manco Ccapac was now very old. Feeling the approach of death, and fearing that in leaving the sovereignty to his son, Sinchi Rocca, he and his successors might not be able to retain it owing to the bad things he had done and to the tyranny he had established, he ordered that the ten lineages or companies that had come with him from Tampu-tocco should form themselves into a garrison or guard, to be always on the watch over the persons of his son and of his other descendants to keep them safe. They were to elect the successor when he had been nominated by his father, or succeeded on the death of his father. For he would not trust the natives to nominate or elect, knowing the evil he had done, and the force he had used towards them. Manco Ccapac being now on the point of death, he left the bird indi enclosed in its cage, the tupac-yauri[57] or sceptre, the napa and the suntur-paucar the insignia of a prince, [though tyrant,] to his son Sinchi Rocca that he might take his place, [and this without the consent or election of any of the natives].

[Note 57: Tupac-yauri The sceptre of the sovereign. Molina, pp. 25, 40, 41. Yamqui Pachacuti, p. 92.]

Thus died Manco Ccapac, according to the accounts of those of his ayllu or lineage, at the age of 144 years, which were divided in the following manner. When he set out from Paccari-tampu or

Tampu-tocco he was 36 years of age. From that time until he arrived at the valley of Cuzco, during which interval he was seeking for fertile lands, there were eight years. For in one place he stayed one, in another two years, in others more or less until he reached Cuzco, where he lived all the rest of the time, which was 100 years, as Ccapac or supreme and rich sovereign.

They say that he was a man of good stature, thin, rustic, cruel though frank, and that in dying he was converted into a stone of a height of a vara and a half. The stone was preserved with much veneration in the Ynti-cancha until the year 1559 when, the licentiate Polo Ondegardo being Corregidor of Cuzco, found it and took it away from where it was adored and venerated by all the Incas, in the village of Bimbilla near Cuzco.

From this Manco Ccapac were originated the ten ayllus mentioned above. From his time began the idols huaquis, which was an idol or demon chosen by each Inca for his companion and oracle which gave him answers[58]. That of Manco Ccapac was the bird indi already mentioned. This Manco Ccapac ordered, for the preservation of his memory, the following: His eldest son by his legitimate wife, who was his sister, was to succeed to the sovereignty. If there was a second son his duty was to be to help all the other children and relations. They were to recognize him as the head in all their necessities, and he was to take charge of their interests, and for this duty estates were set aside. This party or lineage was called ayllu If there was no second son, or if there was one who was incapable, the duty was to be passed on to the nearest and ablest relation. And that those to come might have a precedent or example, Manco Ccapac made the first ayllu and called it Chima Panaca Ayllu, which means the lineage descending from Chima, because the first to whom he left his ayllu or lineage in charge was named Chima, and Panaca means "to descend." It is to be noted that the members of this ayllu always adored the statue of Manco Ccapac, and not those of the other Incas, but the ayllus of the other Incas always worshipped that statue and the others also. It is not known what was done with the body, for there was only the statue. They carried it in their wars, thinking that it secured the victories they won. They also took it to Huanacauri, when they celebrated the huarachicos of the Incas. Huayna Ccapac took it with him to Quito and Cayambis, and afterwards it was brought back to Cuzco with the dead body of that Inca. There are still those of this ayllu in Cuzco who preserve the memory of the deeds of Manco Ccapac. The principal heads of the ayllu are now Don Diego Chaco, and Don Juan Huarhua Chima. They are Hurin-cuzcos. Manco Ccapac died in the year 665 of the nativity of Christ our Lord, Loyba the Goth reigning in Spain, Constantine IV being Emperor. He lived in the Ynti-cancha, House of the Sun.

[Note 58: Sarmiento says that every sovereign Inca had a familiar demon or idol which he called guauqui, and that the guauqui of Manco Ccapac was the indi or bird already mentioned. This is corroborated by Polo de Ondegardo. The word seems to be the same as Huauqui, a brother.]

XV.COMMENCES THE LIFE OF SINCHI ROCCA, THE SECOND INCA.

It has been said that Manco Ccapac, the first Inca, who tyrannized over the natives of the valley of Cuzco, only subjugated the Huallas, Alcabisas, Sauaseras, Culunchima, Copalimayta and the others mentioned above, who were all within the circuit of what is now the city of Cuzco.

To this Manco Ccapac succeeded his son Sinchi Rocca, son also of Mama Occlo, his mother and aunt[59]. He succeeded by nomination of his father, under the care of the ayllus who then all lived together, but not by election of the people, they were all either in flight, prisoners, wounded or banished, and were all his mortal enemies owing to the cruelties and robberies exercised upon them by his father Manco Ccapac. Sinchi Rocca was not a warlike person, and no feats of arms are recorded of him, nor did he sally forth from Cuzco, either himself or by his captains[60]. He added nothing to what his father had subjugated, only holding by his ayllus those whom his father had crushed. He had for a wife Mama Cuca of the town of Saño by whom he had a son named Lloqui Yupanqui. Lloqui means left-handed, because he was so. He left his ayllu called Raura Panaca Ayllu of the Hurin-cuzco side. There are some of this ayllu living, the chiefs being Don Alonso Puscon and Don Diego Quispi. These have the duty of knowing and maintaining the things and memories of Sinchi Rocca. He lived in Ynti-cancha, the House of the Sun, and all his years were 127. He succeeded when 108, and reigned 19 years. He died in the year of the nativity of our Lord Jesus Christ 675, Wamba being King of Spain, Leo IV Emperor, and Donus Pope. He left an idol of stone shaped like a fish called Huanachiri Amaru, which during life was his idol or guauqui. Polo, being Corregidor of Cuzco, found this idol, with the body of Sinchi Rocca, in the village of Bimbilla, among some bars of copper. The idol had attendants and cultivated lands for its service.

[Note 59: All the authorities concur that Sinchi Rocca was the second sovereign of the Inca dynasty, except Montesinos, who makes him the first and calls him Inca Rocca. Acosta has Inguarroca, and Betanzos Chincheroca.]

[Note 60: Cieza de Leon and Garcilasso de la Vega also say that Sinchi Rocca waged no wars. The latter tells us that, by peaceful means, he extended his dominions over the Canchis, as far as Chuncara.]

XVI.THE LIFE OF LLOQUI YUPANQUI, THE THIRD INCA.

On the death of Sinchi Rocca the Incaship was occupied by Lloqui Yupanqui, son of Sinchi Rocca by Mama Cuca his wife. It is to be noted that, although Manco Ccapac had ordered that the eldest son should succeed, this Inca broke the rule of his grandfather, for he had an elder brother named Manco Sapaca[61], as it is said, who did not consent, and the Indians do not declare whether he was nominated by his father. From this I think that Lloqui Yupanqui was not nominated, but Manco Sapaca as the eldest, for so little regard for the natives or their approval was shown. This being so, it was tyranny against the natives and infidelity to relations with connivance of the ayllus legionaries; and with the Inca's favour they could do what they liked, by supporting him. So Lloqui Yupanqui lived in Ynti-cancha like his father[62]. He never left Cuzco on a warlike expedition nor performed any memorable deed, but merely lived like his father, having communication with some provinces and chiefs. These were Huaman Samo, chief of Huaro, Pachaculla Viracocha, the Ayamarcas of Tampu-cunca, and the Quilliscachis[63].

[Note 61: Manco Sapaca, the eldest son of Sinchi Rocca, is also mentioned by Balboa, pp. 14, 20, 22.]

[Note 62: All the authorities concur in making Lloqui Yupanqui the third Inca, except Acosta, who has Iaguarhuaque. Herrera spells it Lloki Yupanqui, Fernandez has Lloccuco Panque, merely corrupt spellings. Cieza de Leon also represents this reign to have been peaceful, but Garcilasso de la Vega makes Lloqui Yupanqui conquer the Collao.]

[Note 63: Huaro or Guaro is a village south of Cuzco in the valley of the Vilcamayu (Balboa, p. 110). Huaman Samo was the chief of Huaro. Balboa mentions Pachachalla Viracocha as a chief of great prudence and ability who submitted to Lloqui Yupanqui, pp. 21, 22. The Ayamarcas formed a powerful tribe about 12 miles south of Cuzco. The Quilliscachis formed one of the original tribes in the valley of Cuzco (Yamqui Pachacuti, p. 110). Tampu-cunca only occurs here.]

One day Lloqui Yupanqui being very sad and afflicted, the Sun appeared to him in the form of a person and consoled him by saying—-"Do not be sorrowful, Lloqui Yupanqui, for from you shall descend great Lords," also, that he might hold it for certain that he would have male issue. For Lloqui Yupanqui was then very old, and neither had a son nor expected to have one. This having been made known, and what the Sun had announced to Lloqui Yupanqui having been published to the people, his relations determined to seek a wife for him. His brother Manco Sapaca, understanding the fraternal disposition, sought for a woman who was suitable for it. He found her in a town called Oma, two leagues from Cuzco, asked for her from her guardians, and, with their consent, brought her to Cuzco. She was then married to Lloqui Yupanqui. Her name was Mama Cava, and by her the Inca had a son named Mayta Ccapac.

This Lloqui did nothing worthy of remembrance. He carried with him an idol, which was his guauqui called Apu Mayta. His ayllu is Avayni Panaca Ayllu, because the first who had the charge of this ayllu was named Avayni. This Inca lived and died in Ynti-cancha. He was 132 years of age, having succeeded at the age of 21, so that he was sovereign or "ccapac" for 111 years. He died in 786, Alfonso el Casto being King of Spain and Leo IV Supreme Pontiff. Some of this ayllu still live at Cuzco. The chiefs are Putisuc Titu Avcaylli, Titu Rimachi, Don Felipe Titu Cunti Mayta, Don Agustin Cunti Mayta, Juan Bautista Quispi Cunti Mayta. They are Hurin-cuzcos. The Licentiate Polo found the body of this Inca with the rest.

XVII. THE LIFE OF MAYTA CCAPAC, THE FOURTH INCA[64].

[Note 64: All authorities agree that Mayta Ccapac was the fourth Inca, except Acosta and Betanzos. Acosta has Viracocha. Betanzos places Mayta Ccapac after Ccapac Yupanqui, whom other authorities make his son. His reign was peaceful except that he encountered and finally vanquished the Alcabisas. But Garcilasso de la Vega makes him the conqueror of the region south of lake Titicaca, as well as provinces to the westward, including the settlement of Arequipa. All this is doubtless a mistake on the part of Garcilasso.]

Mayta Ccapac, the fourth Inca, son of Lloqui Yupanqui and his wife Mama Cava, is to those Indians what Hercules is to us, as regards his birth and acts, for they relate strange things of him. At the very first the Indians of his lineage, and all the others in general, say that his father, when he was begotten, was so old and weak that every one believed he was useless, so that they thought the conception was a miracle. The second wonder was that his mother bore him three months after conception, and that he was born strong and with teeth. All affirm this, and that he grew at such a rate that in one year he had as much strength and was as big as a boy of eight years or more. At two years he fought with very big boys, knocked them about and hurt them seriously. This all looks as if it might be counted with the other fables, but I write what the natives believe respecting their ancestors, and they hold this to be so true that they would kill anyone who asserted the contrary.

They say of this Mayta that when he was of very tender years, he was playing with some boys of the Alcabisas and Culunchimas, natives of Cuzco, when he hurt many of them and killed some. And one day, drinking or taking water from a fountain, he broke the leg of the son of a Sinchi of the Alcabisas, and hunted the rest until they shut themselves up in their houses, where the Alcabisas lived without injuring the Incas.

But now the Alcabisas, unable to endure longer the naughtiness of Mayta Ccapac, which he practised under the protection of Lloqui Yupanqui, and the ayllus who watched over him, determined to regain their liberty and to venture their lives for it. So they selected ten resolute Indians to go to the House of the Sun where Lloqui Yupanqui and his son Mayta Ccapac lived, and enter it with the intention of killing them. At the time Mayta Ccapac was in the court yard of the house, playing at ball with some other boys. When he saw enemies entering the house with arms, he threw one of the balls he was playing with, and killed one. He did the same to another, and, attacking the rest, they all fled. Though the rest escaped, they had received many wounds, and in this state they went back to their Sinchis of Calunchima and Alcabasa.

The Chiefs, considering the harm Mayta Ccapac had done to the natives when a child, feared that when he was grown up he would destroy them all, and for this reason they resolved to die for their liberty. All the inhabitants of the valley of Cuzco, that had been spared by Manco Ccapac, united to make war on the Incas. This very seriously alarmed Lloqui Yupanqui. He thought he was lost, and reprehended his son Mayta Ccapac, saying, "Son! why hast thou been so harmful to the natives of this valley, so that in my old age I shall die at the hands of our enemies?" As the ayllus, who were in garrison with the Incas, rejoiced more in rapine and disturbances than in quiet, they took the part of Mayta Ccapac and told the old Inca to hold his peace, leaving the matter to his son, so Lloqui Yupanqui took no further steps in reprehending Mayta Ccapac. The Alcabisas and Culunchimas assembled their forces and Mayta Ccapac marshalled his ayllus. There was a battle between the two armies and although it was doubtful for some time, both sides fighting desperately for victory, the Alcabisas and Calunchimas were finally defeated by the troops of Mayta Ccapac.

But not for this did the Alcabisas give up the attempt to free themselves and avenge their wrongs. Again they challenged Mayta Ccapac to battle, which he accepted. As they advanced they say that such a hail storm fell over the Alcabisas that they were defeated a third time, and entirely broken up. Mayta Ccapac imprisoned their Sinchi for the remainder of his life.

Mayta Ccapac married Mama Tacucaray, native of the town of Tacucaray, and by her he had a legitimate son named Ccapac Yupanqui, besides four others named Tarco Huaman, Apu Cunti Mayta, Queco Avcaylli, and Rocca Yupanqui.

This Mayta Ccapac was warlike, and the Inca who first distinguished himself in arms after the time of Mama Huaco and Manco Ccapac. They relate of him that he dared to open the hamper containing the bird indi. This bird, brought by Manco Ccapac from Tampu-tocco, had been inherited by his successors, the predecessors of Mayta Ccapac, who had always kept it shut up in a hamper or box of straw, such was the fear they had of it. But Mayta Ccapac was bolder than any of them. Desirous of seeing what his predecessors had guarded so carefully, he opened the hamper, saw the bird indi and had some conversation with it. They say that it gave him oracles, and that after the interview with the bird he was wiser, and knew better what he should do, and what would happen.

With all this he did not go forth from the valley of Cuzco, although chiefs from some distant nations came to visit him. He lived in Ynti-cancha, the House of the Sun. He left a lineage called Usca Mayta Panaca Ayllu, and some members of it are still living in Cuzco. The heads are named Don Juan Tambo Usca Mayta, and Don Baltasar Quiso Mayta. They are Hurin-cuzcos. Mayta Ccapac died at the age of 112 years, in the year 890 of the nativity of our Lord Jesus Christ. The Licentiate Polo found his body and idol guauqui with the rest.

XVIII. THE LIFE OF CCAPAC YUPANQUI, THE FIFTH INCA[65].

[Note 65: All authorities are agreed that Ccapac Yupanqui was the fifth Inca, except Betanzos, who puts him in his father's place. Garcilasso attributes extensive conquests to him, both to south and west.]

At the time of his death, Mayta Ccapac named Ccapac Yupanqui as his successor, his son by his wife Mama Tacucaray. This Ccapac Yupanqui, as soon as he succeeded to the Incaship, made his brothers swear allegiance to him, and that they desired that he should be Ccapac. They complied from fear, for he was proud and cruel. At first he lived very quietly in the Ynti-cancha. It is to be noted that although Ccapac Yupanqui succeeded his father, he was not the eldest son. Cunti Mayta, who was older, had an ugly face. His father had, therefore, disinherited him and named Ccapac Yupanqui as successor to the sovereignty, and Cunti Mayta as high priest. For this reason Ccapac Yupanqui was not the legitimate heir, although he tyrannically forced his brothers to swear allegiance to him.

This Inca, it is said, was the first to make conquests beyond the valley of Cuzco. He forcibly subjugated the people of Cuyumarca and Ancasmarca, four leagues from Cuzco. A wealthy Sinchi of Ayamarca, from fear, presented his daughter, named Ccuri-hilpay to the Inca. Others say that she was a native of Cuzco. The Inca received her as his wife, and had a son by her named Inca Rocca, besides five other sons by various women. These sons were named Apu Calla, Humpi, Apu Saca, Apu Chima-chaui, and Uchun-cuna-ascalla-rando[66]. Apu Saca had a son named Apu Mayta, a very valiant and famous captain, who greatly distinguished himself in the time of Inca Rocca and Viracocha Inca, in company with Vicaquirau, another esteemed captain. Besides these Ccapac Yupanqui had another son named Apu Urco Huaranca[67]. This Ccapac Yupanqui lived 104 years, and was Ccapac for 89 years. He succeeded at the age of 15, and died in the year 980 of the nativity of our redeemer Jesus Christ. His ayllu or lineage was and is called Apu Mayta Panaca Ayllu. Several of this lineage are now living, the principal heads being four in number, namely, Don Cristobal Cusi-hualpa, Don Antonio Piçuy, Don Francisco Cocasaca, and Don Alonso Rupaca. They are Hurin-cuzcos. The Licentiate Polo found the idol or guaoqui of this Inca with the body. They were hidden with the rest, to conceal the idolatrous ceremonies of heathen times.

[Note 66: Calla means a distaff. Humpi means perspiration. Saca is a game bird, also a comet. Chima-chaui is a proper name with no meaning. The name of the fifth son is rather unmanageable. Uchun-cuna-ascalla-rando. Uchun-cuna would mean the Peruvian pepper with the plural particle. Ascalla would be a small potato. Rando is a corrupt form of runtu, an egg. This little Inca seems to have done the marketing.]

[Note 67: Urco, the male gender. Huaranca, a thousand.]

XIX. THE LIFE OF INCA ROCCA, THE SIXTH INCA[68].

When Ccapac Yupanqui died, Inca Rocca, his son by his wife Ccuri-hilpay, succeeded by nomination of his father and the guardian ayllus. This Inca Rocca showed force and valour at the beginning of his Incaship, for he conquered the territories of Muyna[69] and Pinahua with great violence and cruelty. They are rather more than four leagues to the south-south-east of Cuzco. He killed their Sinchis Muyna Pancu, and Huaman-tupac, though some say that Huaman-tupac fled and was never more seen. He did this by the help of Apu Mayta his nephew, and grandson of Ccapac Yupanqui. He also conquered Caytomarca, four leagues from Cuzco. He discovered the waters of Hurin-chacan and those of Hanan-chacan, which is as much as to say the upper and lower waters of Cuzco, and led them in conduits; so that to this day they irrigate fields; and his sons and descendants have benefited by them to this day.

[Note 68: All authorities are agreed respecting Inca Rocca as the sixth Inca. Garcilasso makes him extend the Inca dominion beyond the Apurimac, and into the country of the Chancos.]

[Note 69: Muyna is a district with a lake, 14 miles S.S.W. of Cuzco. Pinahua is mentioned by Garcilasso as a chief to the westward, i. p. 71.]

Inca Rocca gave himself up to pleasures and banquets, preferring to live in idleness. He loved his children to that extent, that for them he forgot duties to his people and even to his own person.

He married a great lady of the town of Pata-huayllacan, daughter of the Sinchi of that territory, named Soma Inca. Her name was Mama Micay. From this marriage came the wars between Tocay Ccapac and the Cuzcos as we shall presently relate. By this wife Inca Rocca had a son named Titu Cusi Hualpa[70], and by another name Yahuar-huaccac, and besides this eldest legitimate son he had four other famous sons named Inca Paucar, Huaman Taysi Inca, and Vicaquirau Inca[70]. The latter was a great warrior, companion in arms with Apu Mayta. These two captains won great victories and subdued many provinces for Viracocha Inca and Inca Yupanqui. They were the founders of the great power to which the Incas afterwards attained. [Note 70: Titu means august or magnanimous. Cusi joyful. Hualpa a game bird. Paucar means beautiful or bright coloured. Huaman a falcon. Vica may be nilca sacred. Quirau a cradle.]

As the events which happened in the reign of Inca Rocca touching the Ayamarcas will be narrated in the life of his son, we will not say more of this Inca, except that, while his ancestors had always lived in the lower part of Cuzco, and were therefore called Hurin-cuzcos, he ordered that those who sprang from him should form another party, and be called Hanan-cuzcos, which means the Cuzcos of the upper part. So that from this Inca began the party of upper or Hanan-cuzcos, for presently he and his successors left their residence at the House of the Sun, and established themselves away from it, building palaces where they lived, in the upper part of the town. It is to be noted that each Inca had a special palace in which he lived, the son not wishing to reside in the palace where his father had lived. It was left in the same state as it was in when the father died, with servants, relations, ayllus or heirs that they might maintain it, and keep the edifices in repair. The Incas and their ayllus were, and still are Hanan-cuzco; although afterwards, in the time of Pachacuti, these ayllus were reformed by him. Some say that then were established the two parties which have been so celebrated in these parts.

Inca Rocca named his son Vicaquirao as the head of his lineage, and it is still called after him the Vicaquirao Panaca Ayllu. There are now some of this lineage living in Cuzco, the principal heads who protect and maintain it being the following: Don Francisco Huaman Rimachi Hachacoma, and Don Antonio Huaman Mayta. They are Hanan-cuzcos. Inca Rocca lived 103 years, and died in the year 1088 of the nativity of our Lord. The Licentiate Polo found his body in the town called Rarapa, kept there with much care and veneration according to their rites.

XX. THE LIFE OF TITU CUSI HUALPA, VULGARLY CALLED YAHUAR-HUACCAC.

Titu Cusi Hualpa Inca, eldest son of Inca Rocca and his wife Mama Micay, had a strange adventure in his childhood[71]. These natives therefore relate his life from his childhood, and in the course of it they tell some things of his father, and of some who were strangers in Cuzco, as follows. It has been related how the Inca Rocca married Mama Micay by the rites of their religion. But it must be understood that those of Huayllacan had already promised to give Mama Micay, who was their countrywoman and very beautiful, in marriage to Tocay Ccapac, Sinchi of the Ayamarcas their neighbours. When the Ayamarcas[72] saw that the Huayllacans had broken their word, they were furious and declared war, considering them as enemies. War was carried on, the Huayllacans defending themselves and also attacking the Ayamarcas, both sides committing cruelties, inflicting deaths and losses, and causing great injury to each other. While this war was being waged, Mama Micay gave birth to her son Titu Cusi Hualpa. The war continued for some years after his birth, when both sides saw that they were destroying each other, and agreed to come to terms, to avoid further injury. The Ayamarcas, who were the most powerful, requested those of Huayllacan to deliver the child Titu Cusi Hualpa into their hands, to do what they liked with him. On this condition they would desist from further hostilities, but if it was not complied with, they announced that they would continue a mortal war to the end. The Huayllacans, fearing this, and knowing their inability for further resistance, accepted the condition, although they were uncles and relations of the child. In order to comply it was necessary for them to deceive the Inca. There was, in the town of Paulo, a brother of Inca Rocca and uncle of Titu Cusi Hualpa named Inca Paucar. He went or sent messengers to ask Inca Rocca to think well of sending his nephew Titu Cusi Hualpa to his town of Paulo in order that, while still a child, he might learn to know and care for his relations on his mother's side, while they wanted to make him the heir of their estates. Believing in these words the Inca Rocca consented that his son should be taken to Paulo, or the town of Micocancha. As soon as they had the child in their town the Huayllacans made great feasts in honour of Titu Cusi Hualpa, who was then eight years old, a little more or less. His father had sent some Incas to guard him. When the festivities were over, the Huayllacans sent to give notice to the Ayamarcas that, while they were occupied in ploughing certain lands which they call chacaras, they might come down on the town and carry off the child, doing with him what they chose, in accordance with the agreement. The Ayamarcas, being informed, came at the time and to the place notified and, finding the child Titu Cusi Hualpa alone, they carried it off.

[Note 71: The very interesting story of the kidnapping of the heir of Inca Rocca, is well told by Sarmiento.]

[Note 72: The Ayarmarcas seem to have occupied the country about 15 miles S.S.W. of Cuzco, near Muyna. The word Ayar is the same as that in the names of the brethren of Manco Ccapac. But others omit the r, and make it Ayamarca, Cieza de Leon, pp. 114, 115, Garcilasso, i. p. 80, Yamqui Pachacuti, p. 90. The month of October was called Ayamarca-Raymi. Molina says that it was because the Ayamarca tribe celebrated the feast of Huarachicu in that month.]

Others say that this treason was carried out in another way. While the uncle was giving the child many presents, his cousins, the sons of Inca Paucar, became jealous and treated with Tocay Ccapac to deliver the child into his hands. Owing to this notice Tocay Ccapac came. Inca Paucar had gone out to deliver to his nephew a certain estate and a flock of llamas. Tocay Ccapac, the enemy of Inca Rocca was told by those who had charge of the boy. He who carried him fled, and the boy was seized and carried off by Tocay Ccapac.

Be it the one way or the other, the result was that the Ayamarcas took Titu Cusi Hualpa from the custody of Inca Paucar in the town of Paulo, while Inca Paucar and the Huayllacans sent the news to Inca Rocca by one party, and with another took up arms against the Ayamarcas.

XXI.WHAT HAPPENED AFTER THE AYAMARCAS HAD STOLEN TITU CUSI HUALPA.

When the Ayamarcas and their Sinchi Tocay Ccapac stole the son of Inca Rocca, they marched off with him. The Huayllacans of Paulopampa, under their Sinchi Paucar Inca, marched in pursuit, coming up to them at a place called Amaro, on the territory of the Ayamarcas. There was an encounter between them, one side to recover the child, and the other to keep their capture. But Paucar was only making a demonstration so as to have an excuse ready. Consequently the Ayamarcas were victorious, while the Huayllacans broke and fled. It is said that in this encounter, and when the child was stolen, all the orejones who had come as a guard from Cuzco, were slain. The Ayamarcas then took the child to the chief place of their province called Ahuayro-cancha.

Many say that Tocay Ccapac was not personally in this raid but that he sent his Ayamarcas, who, when they arrived at Ahuayro-cancha, presented the child Titu Cusi Hualpa to him, saying, "Look here, Tocay Ccapac, at the prisoner we have brought you." The Sinchi received his prize with great satisfaction, asking in a loud voice if this was the child of Mama Micay, who ought to have been his wife. Titu Cusi Hualpa, though but a child, replied boldly that he was the son of Mama Micay and of the Inca Rocca. Tocay was indignant when he had heard those words, and ordered those who brought the child as a prisoner to take him out and kill him. The boy, when he heard such a sentence passed upon him, was so filled with sadness and fright, that he began to weep from fear of death. He began to shed tears of blood and with indignation beyond his years, in the form of a malediction he said to Tocay and the Ayamarcas, "I tell you that as sure as you murder me there will come such a curse on you and your descendants that you will all come to an end, without any memory being left of your nation."

The Ayamarcas and Tocay attentively considered this curse of the child together with the tears of blood. They thought there was some great mystery that so young a child should utter such weighty words, and that the fear of death should make such an impression on him that he should shed tears of blood. They were in suspense divining what it portended, whether that the child would become a great man. They revoked the sentence of death, calling the child Yahuar-huaccac, which means "weeper of blood," in allusion to what had taken place.

But although they did not wish to kill him then and with their own hands, they ordered that he should lead such a life as that he would die of hunger. Before this they all said to the child that he should turn his face to Cuzco and weep over it, because those curses he had pronounced, would fall on the inhabitants of Cuzco, and so it happened.

This done they delivered him to the most valiant Indians, and ordered them to take him to certain farms where flocks were kept, giving him to eat by rule, and so sparingly that he would be consumed with hunger before he died. He was there for a year without leaving the place, so that they did not know at Cuzco, or anywhere else, whether he was dead or alive. During this time Inca Rocca, being without certain knowledge of his son, did not wish to make war on the Ayamarcas because, if he was alive, they might kill him. So he did no more than prepare his men of war and keep ready, while he enquired for his son in all the ways that were possible.

XXII. HOW IT BECAME KNOWN THAT YAHUAR-HUACCAC WAS ALIVE.

As the child Yahuar-huaccac was a year among the shepherds without leaving their huts, which served as a prison, no one knew where he was, because he could not come forth, being well watched by the shepherds and other guards. But it so happened that there was a woman in the place called Chimpu Orma, native of the town of Anta, three leagues from Cuzco. She was a concubine of the Sinchi Tocay Ccapac, and for this reason she had leave to walk about and go into all parts as she pleased. She was the daughter of the Sinchi of Anta, and having given an account of the treatment of the child to her father, brothers, and relations, she persuaded them to help in his liberation. They came on a certain day and, with the pass given them by Chimpu Orma, the father and relations arranged the escape of Yahuar-huaccac. They stationed themselves behind a hill. Yahuar-huaccac was to run in a race with some other boys, to see which could get to the top of the hill first. When the prince reached the top, the men of Anta, who were hidden there, took him in their arms and ran swiftly with him to Anta. When the other boys saw this they quickly gave notice to the valiant guards, who ran after the men of Anta. They overtook them at the lake of Huaypon, where there was a fierce battle. Finally the Ayamarcas got the worst of it, for they were nearly all killed or wounded. The men of Anta continued their journey to their town, where they gave many presents to Yahuar-huaccac and much service, having freed him from the mortal imprisonment in which Tocay Ccapac held him. In this town of Anta the boy remained a year, being served with much love, but so secretly that his father Inca Rocca did not know that he had escaped, during all that time. At the end of a year those of Anta agreed to send messengers to Inca Rocca to let him know of the safety of his son and heir, because they desired to know and serve him. The messengers went to Inca Rocca and, having delivered their message, received the reply that the Inca only knew that the Ayamarcas had stolen his son. They were asked about it again and again, and at last Inca Rocca came down from his throne and closely examined the messengers, that they might tell him more, for not without cause had he asked them so often. The messengers, being so persistently questioned by Inca Rocca, related what had passed, and that his son was free in Anta, served and regaled by the chief who had liberated him. Inca Rocca rejoiced, promised favours, and dismissed the messengers with thanks. Inca Rocca then celebrated the event with feasts and rejoicings. But not feeling quite certain of the truth of what he had been told, he sent a poor man seeking charity to make enquiries at Anta, whether it was all true. The poor man went, ascertained that the child was certainly liberated, and returned with the news to Inca Rocca; which gave rise to further rejoicings in Cuzco. Presently the Inca sent many principal people of Cuzco with presents of gold, silver, and cloth to the Antas, asking them to receive them and to send back his son. The Antas replied that they did not want his presents which they returned, that they cared more that Yahuar-huaccac should remain with them, that they might serve him and his father also, for they felt much love for the boy. Yet if Inca Rocca wanted his son, he should be returned on condition that, from that time forwards, the Antas should be called relations of the orejones. When Inca Rocca was made acquainted with the condition, he went to Anta and conceded what they asked for, to the Sinchi and his people. For this reason the Antas were called relations of the Cuzcos from that time.

Inca Rocca brought his son Yahuar-huaccac to Cuzco and nominated him successor to the Incaship, the ayllus and orejones receiving him as such. At the end of two years Inca Rocca died, and Yahuar-huaccac, whose former name was Titu Cusi Hualpa, remained sole Inca. Before Inca Rocca died he made friends with Tocay Ccapac, through the mediation of Mama Chicya, daughter of Tocay Ccapac, who married Yahuar-huaccac, and Inca Rocca gave his daughter Ccuri-Occllo in marriage to Tocay Ccapac.

XXIII. YAHUAR-HUACCAC INCA YUPANQUI COMMENCES HIS REIGN ALONE, AFTER THE DEATH OF HIS FATHER[73].

When Yahuar-huaccac found himself in possession of the sole sovereignty, he remembered the treason with which he had been betrayed by the Huayllacans who sold him and delivered him up to his enemies the Ayamarcas; and he proposed to inflict an exemplary punishment on them. When the Huayllacans knew this, they humbled themselves before Yahuar-huaccac, entreating him to forgive the evil deeds they had committed against him. Yahuar-huaccac, taking into consideration that they were relations, forgave them. Then he sent a force, under the command of his brother Vicaquirau, against Mohina and Pinahua, four leagues from Cuzco, who subdued these places. He committed great cruelties, for no other reason than that they did not come to obey his will. This would be about 23 years after the time when he rested in Cuzco. Some years afterwards the town of Mollaca, near Cuzco, was conquered and subjugated by force of arms. [Note 73: Yahuar means blood. Huaccani to weep. Yahuar-huaccac succeeded to Inca Rocca according to Garcilasso de la Vega, Montesinos, Betanzos, Balboa, Yamqui Pachacuti and

Sarmiento. Cieza de Leon and Herrera have Inca Yupanqui. Garcilasso makes this Inca banish his son Viracocha, who returns in consequence of a dream, and defeats the Chancas. This all seems to be a mistake. It was Viracocha who fled, and his son Inca Yupanqui, surnamed Pachacuti, who defeated the Chancas and dethroned his father.]

Yahuar-huaccac had, by his wife Mama Chicya, three legitimate sons. The eldest was Paucar Ayllu. The second, Pahuac Hualpa Mayta[74], was chosen to succeed his father, though he was not the eldest. The third was named Viracocha, who was afterwards Inca through the death of his brother. Besides these he had three other illegitimate sons named Vicchu Tupac because he subdued the town of Vicchu, Marca-yutu, and Rocca Inca. As the Huayllacans wanted Marca-yutu to succeed Yahuar-huaccac, because he was their relation, they determined to kill Pahuac Hualpa Mayta, who was nominated to succeed. With this object they asked his father to let him go to Paulo. Forgetting their former treason, he sent the child to its grandfather Soma Inca with forty orejones of the ayllus of Cuzco as his guard. When he came to their town they killed him, for which the Inca, his father, inflicted a great punishment on the Huayllacans, killing some and banishing others until very few were left.

[Note 74: Or Pahuac Mayta Inca (Garcilasso de la Vega, i. p. 23) so named from his swiftness. Pahuani, to run.]

The Inca then went to the conquest of Pillauya, three leagues from Cuzco in the valley of Pisac, and to Choyca, an adjacent place, and to Yuco. After that he oppressed by force and with cruelties, the towns of Chillincay, Taocamarca, and the Caviñas, making them pay tribute. The Inca conquered ten places himself or through his son and captains. Some attribute all the conquests to his son Viracocha.

This Inca was a man of gentle disposition and very handsome face. He lived 115 years. He succeeded his father at the age of 19, and was sovereign for 96 years. He left an ayllu named Aucaylli Panaca, and some are still living at Cuzco. The principal chiefs who maintain it are Don Juan Concha Yupanqui, Don Martin Titu Yupanqui, and Don Gonzalo Paucar Aucaylli. They are Hanan-cuzcos. The body of this Inca has not been discovered[75]. It is believed that those of the town of Paulo have it, with the Inca's guauqui.

[Note 75: In the margin of the MS., "The witnesses said that they believed that the licentiate Polo found it." Navamuel.]

XXIV.LIFE OF VIRACOCHA THE EIGHTH INCA[76].

[Note 76: All authorities agree respecting Viracocha as the eighth Inca.]

As the Huayllacans murdered Pahuac Hualpa Mayta who should have succeeded his father Yahuar-huaccac, the second son Viracocha Inca was nominated for the succession, whose name when a child was Hatun Tupac Inca, younger legitimate son of Yahuar-huaccac and Mama Chicya. He was married to Mama Runtucaya, a native of Anta. Once when this Hatun Tupac Inca was in Urcos, a town which is a little more than five leagues S.S.E. of Cuzco, where there was a sumptuous huaca in honour of Ticci Viracocha, the deity appeared to him in the night. Next morning he assembled his orejones, among them his tutor Hualpa Rimachi, and told them how Viracocha had appeared to him that night, and had announced great good fortune to him and his descendants. In congratulating him Hualpa Rimachi saluted him, "O Viracocha Inca." The rest followed his example and celebrated this name, and the Inca retained it all the rest of his life. Others say that he took this name, because, when he was armed as a knight and had his ears bored, he took Ticci Viracocha as the godfather of his knighthood. Be it as it may, all that is certain is that when a child, before he succeeded his father, he was named Hatun Tupac Inca, and afterwards, for the rest of his life, Viracocha Inca.

After he saw the apparition in Urcos, the Inca came to Cuzco, and conceived the plan of conquering and tyrannizing over all the country that surrounds Cuzco. For it is to be understood that, although his father and grandfather had conquered and robbed in these directions, as their only object was rapine and bloodshed, they did not place garrisons in the places they subdued, so that when the Inca, who had conquered these people, died, they rose in arms and regained their liberty. This is the reason that we repeat several times that a place was conquered, for it was by different Incas. For instance Mohina and Pinahua, although first overrun by Inca Rocca, were also invaded by Yahuar-huaccac, and then by Viracocha and his son Inca Yupanqui. Each town fought so hard for its liberty, both under their Sinchis and without them, that one succeeded in subjugating one and another defeated another. This was especially the case in the time of the Incas. Even in Cuzco itself those of one suburb, called Carmenca, made war on another suburb called Cayocachi. So it is to be understood that, in the time of the seven Incas preceding Viracocha, although owing to the power they possessed in the ayllus, they terrorized those of Cuzco and the immediate neighbourhood, the subjection only lasted while the lance was over the vanquished, and that the moment they had a chance they took up arms for their liberty. They did this at great risk to themselves, and sustained much loss of life, even those in Cuzco itself, until the time of Viracocha Inca.

This Inca had resolved to subjugate all the tribes he possibly could by force and cruelty. He selected as his captains two valiant orejones the one named Apu Mayta and the other Vicaquirau, of the lineage of Inca Rocca. With these captains, who were cruel and impious, he began to subjugate, before all things, the inhabitants of Cuzco who were not Incas orejones, practising on them great cruelties and putting many to death. At this time many towns and provinces were up in arms. Those in the neighbourhood of Cuzco had risen to defend themselves from the orejones Incas of Cuzco who had made war to tyrannize over them. Others were in arms with the same motives as the Incas, which was to subdue them if their forces would suffice. Thus it was that though many Sinchis were elected, their proceedings were confused and without concert, so that each force was small, and they were all weak and without help from each other. This being known to Viracocha, it encouraged him to commence his policy of conquest beyond Cuzco.

Before coming to treat of the nations which Viracocha Inca conquered, we will tell of the sons he had. By Mama Runtucaya, his legitimate wife, he had four sons, the first and eldest Inca Rocca, the second Tupac Yupanqui, the third Inca Yupanqui, and the fourth Ccapac Yupanqui. By another beautiful Indian named Ccuri-chulpa, of the Ayavilla nation in the valley of Cuzco he also had two sons, the one named Inca Urco, the other Inca Socso. The descendants of Inca Urco, however, say that he was legitimate, but all the rest say that he was a bastard[77].
[Note 77: Urco is made by Cieza de Leon to succeed, and to have been dethroned by Inca Yupanqui owing to his flight from the Chancas. Yamqui Pachacuti records the death of Urco. Herrera, Fernandez, Yamqui Pachacuti also make Urco succeed Viracocha.]

XXV. THE PROVINCES AND TOWNS CONQUERED BY THE EIGHTH INCA VIRACOCHA.

Viracocha, having named Apu Mayta and Vicaquirau as his captains, and mustered his forces, gave orders that they should advance to make conquests beyond the valley of Cuzco. They went to Pacaycacha, in the valley of Pisac, three leagues and a half from Cuzco. And because the besieged did not submit at once they assaulted the town, killing the inhabitants and their Sinchi named Acamaqui. Next the Inca marched against the towns of Mohina, Pinahua, Casacancha, and Runtucancha, five short leagues from Cuzco. They had made themselves free, although Yahuar-huaccac had sacked their towns. The captains of Viracocha attacked and killed most of the natives, and their Sinchis named Muyna Pancu and Huaman Tupac. The people of Mohina and Pinahua suffered from this war and subsequent cruelties because they said that they were free, and would not serve nor be vassals to the Incas.

At this time the eldest son, Inca Rocca, was grown up and showed signs of being a courageous man. Viracocha, therefore, made him captain-general with Apu Mayta and Vicaquirau as his colleagues. They also took with them Inca Yupanqui, who also gave hopes owing to the valour he had shown in the flower of his youth. With these captains the conquests were continued. Huaypar-marca was taken, the Ayamarcas were subdued, and Tocay Ccapac and Chihuay Ccapac, who had their seats near Cuzco, were slain. The Incas next subjugated Mollaca and ruined the town of Cayto, four leagues from Cuzco, killing its Sinchi named Ccapac Chani They assaulted the towns of Socma and Chiraques, killing their Sinchis named Puma Lloqui and Illacumbi, who were very warlike chiefs in that time, who had most valorously resisted the attacks of former Incas, that they might not come from Cuzco to subdue them. The Inca captains also conquered Calca and Caquia Xaquixahuana, three leagues from Cuzco, and the towns of Collocte and Camal. They subdued the people between Cuzco and Quiquisana with the surrounding country, the Papris and other neighbouring places; all within seven or eight leagues round Cuzco. [In these conquests they committed very great cruelties, robberies, put many to death and destroyed towns, burning and desolating along the road without leaving memory of anything.]

As Viracocha was now very old, he nominated as his successor his bastard son Inca Urco, without regard to the order of succession, because he was very fond of his mother. This Inca was bold, proud, and despised others, so that he aroused the indignation of the warriors, more especially of the legitimate sons, Inca Rocca, who was the eldest, and of the valiant captains Apu Mayta and Vicaquirau. These took order to prevent this succession to the Incaship, preferring one of the other brothers, the best conditioned, who would treat them well and honourably as they deserved. They secretly set their eyes on the third of the legitimate sons named Cusi, afterwards called Inca Yupanqui, because they believed that he was mild and affable, and, besides these qualities, he showed signs of high spirit and lofty ideas. Apu Mayta was more in favour of this plan than the others, as he desired to have some one to shield him from the fury of Viracocha Inca. Mayta thought that the Inca would kill him because he had seduced a woman named Cacchon Chicya, who was a wife of Viracocha. Apu Mayta had spoken of his plan and of his devotion to Cusi, to his colleague Vicaquirau. While they were consulting how it should be managed, the Chancas of Andahuaylas, thirty leagues from Cuzco, marched upon that city, as will be narrated in the life of Inca Yupanqui. Inca Viracocha, from fear of them, fled from Cuzco, and went to a place called Caquia Xaquixahuana, where he shut himself up, being afraid of the Chancas. Here he died after some years, deprived of Cuzco of which his son Cusi had possession for several years before his father's death. Viracocha Inca was he who had made the most extensive conquests beyond Cuzco and, as we may say, he tyrannized anew even as regards Cuzco, as has been said above.

Viracocha lived 119 years, succeeding at the age of 18. He was Ccapac 101 years. He named the ayllu, which he left for the continuance of his lineage, Socso Panaca Ayllu, and some are still living at Cuzco, the heads being Amaru Titu, Don Francisco Chalco Yupanqui, Don Francisco Anti Hualpa. They are Hanan-cuzcos.

This Inca was industrious, and inventor of cloths and embroidered work called in their language Viracocha-tocapu, and amongst us brocade. He was rich [for he robbed much] and had vases of gold and silver. He was buried in Caquia Xaquixahuana and Gonzalo Pizarro, having heard that there was treasure with the body, discovered it and a large sum of gold. He burnt the body, and the natives collected the ashes and hid them in a vase. This, with the Inca's guauqui, called Inca Amaru, was found by the Licentiate Polo, when he was Corregidor of Cuzco.

XXVI. THE LIFE OF INCA YUPANQUI OR PACHACUTI[78], THE NINTH INCA.

[Note 78: Inca Yupanqui surnamed Pachacuti was the ninth Inca. All the authorities agree that he dethroned either his father Viracocha, or his half brother Urco, after his victory over the Chancas, and that he had a long and glorious reign.]

It is related, in the life of Inca Viracocha, that he had four legitimate sons. Of these the third named Cusi, and as surname Inca Yupanqui, was raised to the Incaship by the famous captains Apu Mayta and Vicaquirau, and by the rest of the legitimate sons, and against the will of his father. In the course of their intrigues to carry this into effect, the times gave them the opportunity which they could not otherwise have found, in the march of the Chancas upon Cuzco. It happened in this way.

Thirty leagues to the west of Cuzco there is a province called Andahuaylas, the names of the natives of it being Chancas. In this province there were two Sinchis, [robbers and cruel tyrants] named Uscovilca and Ancovilca who, coming on an expedition from near Huamanca with some companies of robbers, had settled in the valley of Andahuaylas, and had there formed a state. They were brothers. Uscovilca being the elder and principal one, instituted a tribe which he called Hanan-chancas or upper Chancas. Ancovilca formed another tribe called Hurin-chancas or lower Chancas. These chiefs, after death, were embalmed, and because they were feared for their cruelties in life, were kept by their people. The Hanan-chancas carried the statue of Uscovilca with them, in their raids and wars. Although they had other Sinchis, they always attributed their success to the statue of Uscovilca, which they called Ancoallo.

The tribes and companies of Uscovilca had multiplied prodigiously in the time of Viracocha. It seemed to them that they were so powerful that no one could equal them, so they resolved to march from Andahuaylas and conquer Cuzco. With this object they elected two Sinchis, one named Asto-huaraca, and the other Tomay-huaraca, one of the tribe of Hanan-chanca, the other of Hurin-chanca. These were to lead them in their enterprise. The Chancas and their Sinchis were proud and insolent. Setting out from Andahuaylas they marched on the way to Cuzco until they reached a place called Ichu-pampa, five leagues west of that city, where they halted for some days, terrifying the neighbourhood and preparing for an advance.

The news spread terror among the orejones of Cuzco, for they doubted the powers of Inca Viracocha, who was now very old and weak. Thinking that the position of Cuzco was insecure, Viracocha called a Council of his sons and captains Apu Mayta and Vicaquirau. These captains said to him—"Inca Viracocha! we have understood what you have proposed to us touching this matter, and how you ought to meet the difficulty. After careful consideration it appears to us that as you are old and infirm owing to what you have undergone in former wars, it will not be well that you should attempt so great a business, dangerous and with victory doubtful, such as that which now presents itself before your eyes. The wisest counsel respecting the course you should adopt is that you should leave Cuzco, and proceed to the place of Chita, and thence to Caquia Xaquixahuana, which is a strong fort, whence you may treat for an agreement with the Chancas." They gave this advice to Viracocha to get him out of Cuzco and give them a good opportunity to put their designs into execution, which were to raise Cusi Inca Yupanqui to the throne. In whatever manner it was done, it is certain that this advice was taken by the Inca Viracocha. He determined to leave Cuzco and proceed to Chita, in accordance with their proposal. But when Cusi Inca Yupanqui found that his father was determined to leave Cuzco, they say that he thus addressed him, "How father can it fit into your heart to accept such infamous advice as to leave Cuzco, city of the Sun and of Viracocha, whose name you have taken, whose promise you hold that you shall be a great lord, you and your descendants." Though a boy, he said this with the animated daring of a man high in honour. The father answered that he was a boy and that he spoke like one, in talking without consideration, and that such words were of no value. Inca Yupanqui replied that he would remain where they would be remembered, that he would not leave Cuzco nor abandon the House of the Sun. They say that all this was planned by the said captains of Viracocha, Apu Mayta and Vicaquirau, to throw those off their guard who might conceive suspicion respecting the remaining of Inca Yupanqui in Cuzco. So Viracocha left Cuzco and went to Chita, taking with him his two illegitimate sons Inca Urco and Inca Socso. His son Inca Yupanqui remained at Cuzco, resolved to defend the city or die in its defence. Seven chiefs remained with him; Inca Rocca his elder and legitimate brother, Apu Mayta, Vicaquirau, Quillis-cacha, Urco Huaranca, Chima Chaui Pata Yupanqui, Viracocha Inca Paucar, and Mircoy-mana the tutor of Inca Yupanqui.

XXVII. COMING OF THE CHANCAS AGAINST CUZCO.

At the time when Inca Viracocha left Cuzco, Asto-huaraca and Tomay-huaraca set out for Ichu-pampa, first making sacrifices and blowing out the lungs of an animal, which they call calpa. This they did not well understand, from what happened afterwards. Marching on towards Cuzco, they arrived at a place called Conchacalla, where they took a prisoner. From him they learnt what was happening at Cuzco, and he offered to guide them there secretly. Thus he conducted them half way. But then his conscience cried out to him touching the evil he was doing. So he fled to Cuzco, and gave the news that the Chancas were resolutely advancing. The news of this Indian, who was a Quillis-cachi of Cuzco, made Viracocha hasten his flight to Chita, whither the Chancas sent their messengers summoning him to surrender, and threatening war if he refused. Others say that these were not messengers but scouts and that Inca Viracocha, knowing this, told them that he knew they were spies of the Chancas, that he did not want to kill them, but that they might return and tell their people that if they wanted anything he was there. So they departed and at the mouth of a channel of water some of them fell and were killed. At this the Chancas were much annoyed. They said that the messengers had been ordered to go to Inca Viracocha, and that they were killed by his captain Quequo Mayta.

While this was proceeding with the messengers of the Chancas, the Chanca army was coming nearer to Cuzco. Inca Yupanqui made great praying to Viracocha and to the Sun to protect the city. One day he was at Susurpuquio in great affliction, thinking over the best plan for opposing his enemies, when there appeared a person in the air like the Sun, consoling him and animating him for the battle. This being held up to him a mirror in which the provinces he would subdue were shown, and told him that he would be greater than any of his ancestors: he was to have no doubt, but to return to the city, because he would conquer the Chancas who were marching on Cuzco. With these words the vision animated Inca Yupanqui. He took the mirror, which he carried with him ever afterwards, in peace or war, and returned to the city, where he began to encourage those he had left there, and some who came from afar[79]. The latter came to look on, not daring to declare for either party, fearing the rage of the conqueror if they should join the conquered side. Inca Yupanqui, though only a lad of 20 or 22 years, provided for everything as one who was about to fight for his life.

[Note 79: Susurpuquio seems to have been a fountain or spring on the road to Xaquixahuana. Molina relates the story of the vision somewhat differently, p. 12. Mrs. Zelia Nuttall thinks that the description of the vision bears such a very strong resemblance to a bas relief found in Guatemala that they must have a common origin.]

While the Inca Yupanqui was thus engaged the Chancas had been marching, and reached a place very near Cuzco called Cusi-pampa, there being nothing between it and Cuzco but a low hill. Here the Quillis-cachi was encountered again. He said that he had been to spy, and that he rejoiced to meet them. This deceiver went from one side to the other, always keeping friends with both, to secure the favour of the side which eventually conquered. The Chancas resumed the march, expecting that there would be no defence. But the Quillis-cachi, mourning over the destruction of his country, disappeared from among the Chancas and went to Cuzco to give the alarm. "To arms! to arms!" he shouted, "Inca Yupanqui. The Chancas are upon you."

At these words the Inca, who was not off his guard, mustered and got his troops in order, but he found very few willing to go forth with him to oppose the enemy, almost all took to the hills to watch the event. With those who were willing to follow, though few in number, chiefly the men of the seven Sinchis, brothers and captains, named above, he formed a small force and came forth to receive the enemy who advanced in fury and without order. The opposing forces advanced towards each other, the Chancas attacking the city in four directions. The Inca Yupanqui sent all the succour he could to the assailed points, while he and his friends advanced towards the statue and standard of Uscovilca, with Asto-huaraca and Tomay-huaraca defending them. Here there was a bloody and desperate battle, one side striving to enter the city, and the other opposing its advance. Those who entered by a suburb called Chocos-chacona were valiantly repulsed by the inhabitants. They say that a woman named Chañan-ccuri-coca here fought like a man, and so valiantly opposed the Chancas that they were obliged to retire. This was the cause that all the Chancas who saw it were dismayed. The Inca Yupanqui meanwhile was so quick and dexterous with his weapon, that those who carried the statue of Uscovilca became alarmed, and their fear was increased when they saw great numbers of men coming down from the hills. They say that these were sent by Viracocha, the creator, as succour for the Inca. The Chancas began to give way, leaving the statue of Uscovilca, and they say even that of Ancovilca. Attacking on two sides, Inca Rocca, Apu Mayta, and Vicaquirau made great havock among the Chancas. Seeing that their only safety was in flight, they turned their backs, and their quickness in running exceeded their fierceness in advancing. The men of Cuzco continued the pursuit, killing and wounding, for more than two leagues, when they desisted. The Chancas returned to Ichu-pampa, and the orejones to Cuzco, having won a great victory and taken a vast amount of plunder which remained in their hands. The Cuzcos rejoiced at this victory won with so little expectation or hope. They honoured Inca Yupanqui with many epithets, especially calling him PACHACUTI, which means "over-turner of the earth," alluding to the land and farms which they looked upon as lost by the coming of the Chancas. For he had made them free and safe again. From that time he was called Pachacuti Inca Yupanqui.

As soon as the victory was secure, Inca Yupanqui did not wish to enjoy the triumph although many tried to persuade him. He wished to give his father the glory of such a great victory. So he collected the most precious spoils, and took them to his father who was in Chita, with a principal orejon named Quillis-cachi Urco Huaranca. By him he sent to ask his father to enjoy that triumph and tread on those spoils of the enemy, a custom they have as a sign of victory. When Quillis-cachi Urco Huaranca arrived before Viracocha Inca, he placed those spoils of the Chancas at his feet with great reverence, saying, "Inca Viracocha! thy son Pachacuti Inca Yupanqui, to whom the Sun has given such a great victory, vanquishing the powerful Chancas, sends me to salute you, and says that, as a good and humble son he wishes you to triumph over your victory and to tread upon these spoils of your enemies, conquered by your hands." Inca Viracocha did not wish to tread on them, but said that his son Inca Urco should do so, as he was to succeed to the Incaship. Hearing this the messenger rose and gave utterance to furious words, saying that he did not come for cowards to triumph by the deeds of Pachacuti. He added that if Viracocha did not wish to receive this recognition from so valiant a son, it would be better that Pachachuti should enjoy the glory for which he had worked. With this he returned to Cuzco, and told Pachacuti what had happened with his father.

XXVIII. THE SECOND VICTORY OF PACHACUTI INCA YUPANQUI OVER THE CHANCAS.

While Pachacuti Inca Yupanqui was sending the spoil to his father, the Chancas were recruiting and assembling more men at Ichu-pampa, whence they marched on Cuzco the first time. The Sinchis Tomay-huaraca and Asto-huaraca began to boast, declaring that they would return to Cuzco and leave nothing undestroyed. This news came to Pachacuti Inca Yupanqui. He received it with courage and, assembling his men, he marched in search of the Chancas. When they heard that the Incas were coming, they resolved to march out and encounter them, but the advance of Pachacuti Inca Yupanqui was so rapid that he found the Chancas still at Ichu-pampa.

As soon as the two forces came in sight of each other, Asto-huaraca, full of arrogance, sent to Inca Yupanqui to tell him that he could see the power of the Chancas and the position they now held. They were not like him coming from the poverty stricken Cuzco, and if he did not repent the past and become a tributary and vassal to the Chancas; Asto-huaraca would dye his lance in an Inca's blood. But Inca Yupanqui was not terrified by the embassy. He answered in this way to the messenger. "Go back brother and say to Asto-huaraca, your Sinchi, that Inca Yupanqui is a child of the Sun and guardian of Cuzco, the city of Ticci Viracocha Pachayachachi, by whose order I am here guarding it. For this city is not mine but his; and if your Sinchi should wish to own obedience to Ticci Viracocha, or to me in His name, he will be honourably received. If your Sinchi should see things in another light, show him that I am here with our friends, and if he should conquer us he can call himself Lord and Inca. But let him understand that no more time can be wasted in demands and replies. God (Ticci Viracocha) will give the victory to whom he pleases."

With this reply the Chancas felt that they had profited little by their boasting. They ran to their arms because they saw Pachacuti closely following the bearer of his reply. The two armies approached each other in Ichu-pampa, encountered, and mixed together, the Chancas thrusting with long lances, the Incas using slings, clubs, axes and arrows, each one defending himself and attacking his adversary. The battle raged for a long time, without advantage on either side. At last Pachacuti made a way to where Asto-huaraca was fighting, attacked him and delivered a blow with his hatchet which cut off the Chanca's head. Tomay-huaraca was already killed. The Inca caused the heads of these two captains to be set on the points of lances, and raised on high to be seen by their followers. The Chancas, on seeing the heads, despaired of victory without leaders. They gave up the contest and sought safety in flight. Inca Yupanqui and his army followed in pursuit, wounding and killing until there was nothing more to do.

This great victory yielded such rich and plentiful spoils, that Pachacuti Inca Yupanqui proposed to go to where his father was, report to him the story of the battle and the victory, and to offer him obedience that he might triumph as if the victory was his own. Loaded with spoil and Chanca prisoners he went to visit his father. Some say that it was at a place called Caquia Xaquixahuana, four leagues from Cuzco, others that it was at Marco, three leagues from Cuzco. Wherever it was, there was a great ceremony, presents being given, called muchanaco[80]. When Pachacuti had given his father a full report, he ordered the spoils of the enemy to be placed at his feet, and asked his father to tread on them and triumph over the victory. But Viracocha Inca, still intent upon having Inca Urco for his successor, desired that the honour offered to him should be enjoyed by his favourite son. He, therefore, did not wish to accept the honours for himself. Yet not wishing to offend the Inca Yupanqui Pachacuti on such a crucial point, he said that he would tread on the spoils and prisoners, and did so. He excused himself from going to triumph at Cuzco owing to his great age, which made him prefer to rest at Caquia Xaquixahuana.

[Note 80: Muchani, I worship. Nacu is a particle giving a reciprocal or mutual meaning, "joint worship."]

With this reply Pachacuti departed for Cuzco with a great following of people and riches. The Inca Urco also came to accompany him, and on the road there was a quarrel in the rear guard between the men of Urco and those of Pachacuti. Others say that it was an ambush laid for his brother by Urco and that they fought. The Inca Pachacuti took no notice of it, and continued his journey to Cuzco, where he was received with much applause and in triumph. Soon afterwards, as one who thought of assuming authority over the whole land and taking away esteem from his father, as he presently did, he began to distribute the spoils, and confer many favours with gifts and speeches. With the fame of these grand doings, people came to Cuzco from all directions and many of those who were at Caquia Xaquixahuana left it and came to the new Inca at Cuzco.

XXIX. THE INCA YUPANQUI ASSUMES THE SOVEREIGNTY AND TAKES THE FRINGE, WITHOUT THE CONSENT OF HIS FATHER.

When the Inca Yupanqui found himself so strong and that he had been joined by so many people, he determined not to wait for the nomination of his father, much less for his death, before he rose with the people of Cuzco with the further intention of obtaining the assent of those without. With this object he caused a grand sacrifice to be offered to the Sun in the Inti-cancha or House of the Sun, and then went to ask the image of the Sun who should be Inca. The oracle of the devil, or perhaps some Indian who was behind to give the answer, replied that Inca Yupanqui Pachacuti was chosen and should be Inca. On this answer being given, all who were present at the sacrifice, prostrated themselves before Pachacuti, crying out "Ccapac Inca Intip Churin," which means "Sovereign Lord Child of the Sun."

Presently they prepared a very rich fringe of gold and emeralds wherewith to crown him. Next day they took Pachacuti Inca Yupanqui to the House of the Sun, and when they came to the image of the Sun, which was of gold and the size of a man, they found it with the fringe, as if offering it of its own will. First making his sacrifices, according to their custom, he came to the image, and the High Priest called out in his language "Intip Apu," which means "Governor of things pertaining to the Sun." With much ceremony and great reverence the fringe was taken from the image and placed, with much pomp, on the forehead of Pachacuti Inca Yupanqui. Then all called his name and hailed him "Intip Churin Inca Pachacuti," or "Child of the Sun Lord, over-turner of the earth." From that time he was called Pachacuti besides his first name which was Inca Yupanqui. Then the Inca presented many gifts and celebrated the event with feasts. [He was sovereign Inca without the consent of his father or of the people, but by those he had gained over to his side by gifts.]

XXX.PACHACUTI INCA YUPANQUI REBUILDS THE CITY OF CUZCO.

As soon as the festivities were over, the Inca laid out the city of Cuzco on a better plan; and formed the principal streets as they were when the Spaniards came. He divided the land for communal, public, and private edifices, causing them to be built with very excellent masonry. It is such that we who have seen it, and know that they did not possess instruments of iron or steel to work with, are struck with admiration on beholding the equality and precision with which the stones are laid, as well as the closeness of the points of junction. With the rough stones it is even more interesting to examine the work and its composition. As the sight alone satisfies the curious, I will not waste time in a more detailed description.

Besides this, Pachacuti Inca Yupanqui, considering the small extent of land round Cuzco suited for cultivation, supplied by art what was wanting in nature. Along the skirts of the hills near villages, and also in other parts, he constructed very long terraces of 200 paces more or less, and 20 to 30 wide, faced with masonry, and filled with earth, much of it brought from a distance. We call these terraces andenes, the native name being sucres. He ordered that they should be sown, and in this way he made a vast increase in the cultivated land, and in provision for sustaining the companies and garrisons.

In order that the precise time of sowing and harvesting might be known, and that nothing might be lost, the Inca caused four poles to be set up on a high mountain to the east of Cuzco, about two varas apart, on the heads of which there were holes, by which the sun entered, in the manner of a watch or astrolabe. Observing where the sun struck the ground through these holes, at the time of sowing and harvest, marks were made on the ground. Other poles were set up in the part corresponding to the west of Cuzco, for the time of harvesting the maize. Having fixed the positions exactly by these poles, they built columns of stone for perpetuity in their places, of the height of the poles and with holes in like places. All round it was ordered that the ground should be paved; and on the stones certain lines were drawn, conforming to the movements of the sun entering through the holes in the columns. Thus the whole became an instrument serving for an annual time-piece, by which the times of sowing and harvesting were regulated. Persons were appointed to observe these watches, and to notify to the people the times they indicated[81].

[Note 81: The pillars at Cuzco to determine the time of the solstices were called Sucanca. The two pillars denoting the beginning of winter, whence the year was measured, were called Pucuy Sucanca. Those notifying the beginning of spring were Chirao Sucanca. Suca means a ridge or furrow and sucani to make ridges: hence sucanca, the alternate light and shadow, appearing like furrows. Acosta says there was a pillar for each month. Garcilasso de la Vega tells us that there were eight on the east, and eight on the west side of Cuzco (i. p. 177) in double rows, four and four, two small between two high ones, 20 feet apart. Cieza de Leon says that they were in the Carmenca suburb (i. p. 325).

To ascertain the time of the equinoxes there was a stone column in the open space before the temple of the Sun in the centre of a large circle. This was the Inti-huatana. A line was drawn across from east to west and they watched when the shadow of the pillar was on the line from sunrise to sunset and there was no shadow at noon. There is another Inti-huatana at Pisac, and another at Hatun-colla. Inti, the Sun God, huatani, to seize, to tie round, Inti-huatana, a sun circle.]

Besides this, as he was curious about the things of antiquity, and wished to perpetuate his name, the Inca went personally to the hill of Tampu-tocco or Paccari-tampu, names for the same thing, and entered the cave whence it is held for certain that Manco Ccapac and his brethren came when they marched to Cuzco for the first time, as has already been narrated. After he had made a thorough inspection, he venerated the locality and showed his feeling by festivals and sacrifices. He placed doors of gold on the window Ccapac-tocco, and ordered that from that time forward the locality should be venerated by all, making it a prayer place and huaca, whither to go to pray for oracles and to sacrifice.

Having done this the Inca returned to Cuzco. He ordered the year to be divided into twelve months, almost like our year. I say almost, because there is some difference, though slight, as will be explained in its place.

He called a general assembly of the oldest and wisest men of Cuzco and other parts, who with much diligence scrutinized and examined the histories and antiquities of the land, principally of the Incas and their forefathers. He ordered the events to be painted and preserved in order, as I explained when I spoke of the method adopted in preparing this history.

XXXI.PACHACUTI INCA YUPANQUI REBUILDS THE HOUSE OF THE SUN AND ESTABLISHES NEW IDOLS IN IT.

Having adorned the city of Cuzco with edifices, streets, and the other things that have been mentioned, Pachacuti Inca Yupanqui reflected that since the time of Manco Ccapac, none of his predecessors had done anything for the House of the Sun. He, therefore, resolved to enrich it with more oracles and edifices to appal ignorant people and produce astonishment, that they might help in the conquest of the whole land which he intended to subdue, and in fact he commenced and achieved the subjugation of a large portion of it He disinterred the bodies of the seven deceased Incas, from Manco Ccapac to Yahuar-huaccac, which were all in the House of the Sun, enriching them with masks, head-dresses called chuco, medals, bracelets, sceptres called yauri or champi[82], and other ornaments of gold. He then placed them, in the order of their seniority, on a bench with a back, richly adorned with gold, and ordered great festivals to be celebrated with representations of the lives of each Inca. These festivals, which are called purucaya[83], were continued for more than four months. Great and sumptuous sacrifices were made to each Inca, at the conclusion of the representation of his acts and life. This gave them such authority that it made all strangers adore them, and worship them as gods. These strangers, when they beheld such majesty, humbled themselves, and put up their hands to worship or mucha as they say. The corpses were held in great respect and veneration until the Spaniards came to this land of Peru.

[Note 82: Champi means a one-handed battle axe (Garcilasso de la Vega, I. lib. ix. cap. 31). Novices received it at the festival of Huarachicu, with the word Auccacunapac, for traitors.]

[Note 83: According to Mossi puruccayan was the general mourning on the death of the Inca.]

Besides these corpses, Pachacuti made two images of gold. He called one of them Viracocha Pachayachachi. It represented the creator, and was placed on the right of the image of the Sun. The other was called Chuqui ylla, representing lightning, placed on the left of the Sun. This image was most highly venerated by all. Inca Yupanqui adopted this idol for his guauqui[84], because he said that it had appeared and spoken in a desert place and had given him a serpent with two heads, to carry about with him always, saying that while he had it with him, nothing sinister could happen in his affairs. To these idols the Inca gave the use of lands, flocks, and servants, especially of certain women who lived in the same House of the Sun, in the manner of nuns. These all came as virgins but few remained without having had connexion with the Inca. At least he was so vicious in this respect, that he had access to all whose looks gave him pleasure, and had many sons.

[Note 84: Huauqui, brother.]

Besides this House, there were some huacas in the surrounding country. These were that of Huanacauri, and others called Anahuarqui, Yauira, Cinga, Picol, Pachatopan[85] [to many they made the accursed sacrifices, which they called Ccapac Cocha, burying children, aged 5 or 6, alive as offerings to the devil, with many offerings of vases of gold and silver].

[Note 85: Anahuarqui was the name of the wife of Tupac Inca
Yupanqui. Yauira may be for Yauirca, a fabulous creature described by
Yamqui Pachacuti. Cinga and Picol do not occur elsewhere. Pachatopan is
no doubt Pacha tupac, beautiful land.]

The Inca, they relate, also caused to be made a great woollen chain of many colours, garnished with gold plates, and two red fringes at the end. It was 150 fathoms in length, more or less. This was used in their public festivals, of which there were four principal ones in the year. The first was called RAYMI or CCAPAC RAYMI, which was when they opened the ears of knights at a ceremony called huarachico. The second was called SITUA resembling our lights of St John[86]. They all ran at midnight with torches to bathe, saying that they were thus left clean of all diseases. The third was called YNTI RAYMI, being the feast of the Sun, known as aymuray. In these feasts they took the chain out of the House of the Sun and all the principal Indians, very richly dressed, came with it, in order, singing, from the House of the Sun to the Great Square which they encircled with the chain. This was called moroy urco[87].

[Note 86: The months and the festivals which took place in each month are given by several authorities. The most correct are those of Polo de Ondegardo and Calancha who agree throughout. Calancha gives the months as received by the first Council of Lima.
22 June—22 July. INTIP RAYMI (Sun Festival). 22 July—22 Aug. CHAHUAR HUARQUIZ—Ploughing month. 22 Aug.—22 Sept. YAPAQUIZ (SITUA or Moon Festival)—Sowing month. 22 Sept.—22 Oct. CCOYA RAYMI—-Expiatory feast. Molina a month behind. 22 Oct.—22 Nov. UMA RAYMI—Month of brewing chicha. 22 Nov.—22 Dec. AYAMARCA—Commemoration of the dead. 22 Dec.—22 Jan. CCAPAC RAYMI (HUARACHICU festival). 22 Jan.—22 Feb. CAMAY—Month of exercises. 22 Feb.—22 March. HATUN POCCOY (great ripening). 22 March—22 April. PACHA POCCOY (MOSOC NINA festival). 22 April—22 May. AYRIHUA (Harvest). 22 May—22 June. AYMURAY (Harvest home).]

[Note 87: The great chain, used at festivals, is called by Sarmiento Muru-urco. See also Molina. Muru means a coloured spot, or a thing of variegated colours. Molina says that it was the house where the chain was kept that was called Muru-urco, as well as the cable. Huasca is another name for a cable (See G. de la Vega, ii. p, 422).]

XXXII.PACHACUTI INCA YUPANQUI DEPOPULATES TWO LEAGUES OF COUNTRY NEAR CUZCO.

After Pachacuti had done what has been described in the city, he turned his attention to the people. Seeing that there were not sufficient lands for sowing, so as to sustain them, he went round the city at a distance of four leagues from it, considering the valleys, situation, and villages. He depopulated all that were within two leagues of the city. The lands of depopulated villages were given to the city and its inhabitants, and the deprived people were settled in other parts. The citizens of Cuzco were well satisfied with the arrangement, for they were given what cost little, and thus he made friends by presents taken from others, and took as his own the valley of Tambo [which was not his].

The news of the enlargement of this city went far and wide, and reached the ears of Viracocha Inca, retired in Caquia Xaquixahuana[88]. He was moved to go and see Cuzco. The Inca Yupanqui went for him, and brought him to Cuzco with much rejoicing. He went to the House of the Sun, worshipped at Huanacauri and saw all the improvements that had been made. Having seen everything he returned to his place at Caquia Xaquixahuana, where he resided until his death, never again visiting Cuzco, nor seeing his son Pachacuti Inca Yupanqui.

[Note 88: This great plain to the north-west of Cuzco, called Xaquixahuana, and Sacsahuana, is now known as Surita. Most of the early writers call it Sacsahuana. Sarmiento always places the word Caquia before the name. Capuchini is to provide, capuchic a purveyor. Hence Capuquey means "my goods," abbreviated to Caguey, "my property." The meaning is "my estate of Xaquixahuana."]

XXXIII.PACHACUTI INCA YUPANQUI KILLS HIS ELDER BROTHER NAMED INCA URCO.

Pachacuti Inca Yupanqui found himself so powerful with the companies he had got together by liberal presents to all, that he proposed to subjugate by their means all the territories he could reach. For this he mustered all the troops that were in Cuzco, and provided them with arms, and all that was necessary for war. Affairs being in this state Pachacuti heard that his brother Urco was in a valley called Yucay, four leagues from Cuzco, and that he had assembled some people. Fearing that the movement was intended against him the Inca marched there with his army. His brother Inca Rocca went with him, who had the reputation of being a great necromancer.

Arriving at a place called Paca in the said valley, the Inca went out against his brother Urco, and there was a battle between them. Inca Rocca hurled a stone which hit Urco on the throat. The blow was so great that Urco fell into the river flowing down the ravine where they were fighting. Urco exerted himself and fled, swimming down the river, with his axe in his hand. In this way he reached a rock called Chupellusca, a league below Tampu, where his brothers overtook him and killed him.

From thence the Inca Pachacuti Yupanqui, with his brother Inca Rocca marched with their troops to Caquia Xaquixahuana to see his father who refused ever to speak with or see him, owing to the rage he felt at the death of Inca Urco. But Inca Rocca went in, where Viracocha was and said, "Father! it is not reasonable that you should grieve so much at the death of Urco, for I killed him in self defence, he having come to kill me. You are not to be so heavy at the death of one, when you have so many sons. Think no more of it, for my brother Pachacuti Yupanqui is to be Inca, and I hold that you should favour him and be as a father to him." Seeing the resolution of his son Inca Rocca, Viracocha did not dare to reply or to contradict him. He dismissed him by saying that that was what he wished, and that he would be guided by him in everything. With this the Inca Yupanqui and his brother Inca Rocca returned to Cuzco, and entered the city triumphing over the past victories and over this one.

The triumph was after this manner. The warriors marched in order, in their companies, dressed in the best manner possible, with songs and dances, and the captives, their eyes on the ground, dressed in long robes with many tassels. They entered by the streets of the city, which were very well adorned to receive them. They went on, enacting their battles and victories, on account of which they triumphed. On reaching the House of the Sun, the spoils and prisoners were thrown on the ground, and the Inca walked over them, trampling on them and saying—"I tread on my enemies." The prisoners were silent without raising their eyes. This order was used in all their triumphs. At the end of a short time Inca Viracocha died of grief at the death of Inca Urco, deprived and despoiled of all honour and property. They buried his body in Caquia Xaquixahuana.

XXXIV. THE NATIONS WHICH PACHACUTI INCA SUBJUGATED AND THE TOWNS HE TOOK: AND FIRST OF TOCAY CCAPAC, SINCHI OF THE AYAMARCAS, AND THE DESTRUCTION OF THE CUYOS.

Near Cuzco there is a nation of Indians called Ayamarcas who had a proud and wealthy Sinchi named Tocay Ccapac. Neither he nor his people wished to come and do reverence to the Inca. On the contrary, he mustered his forces to attack the Inca if his country was invaded. This being known to Inca Yupanqui, he assembled his ayllus and other troops. He formed them into two parties, afterwards called Hanan-cuzcos and Hurin-cuzcos, forming them into a corps, that united no one might be able to prevail against them. This done he consulted over what should be undertaken. It was resolved that all should unite for the conquest of all neighbouring nations. Those who would not submit were to be utterly destroyed; and first Tocay Ccapac, chief of the Ayamarcas, was to be dealt with, being powerful and not having come to do homage at Cuzco. Having united his forces, the Inca marched against the Ayamarcas and their Sinchi, and there was a battle at Huanancancha. Inca Yupanqui was victorious, assaulting the villages and killing nearly all the Ayamarcas. He took Tocay Ccapac as a prisoner to Cuzco, where he remained in prison until his death.

After this Inca Yupanqui took to wife a native of Choco named Mama Anahuarqui. For greater pleasure and enjoyment, away from business, he went to the town of the Cuyos, chief place of the province of Cuyo-suyu. Being one day at a great entertainment, a potter, servant of the Sinchi, without apparent reason, threw a stone or, as some say, one of the jars which they call ulti, at the Inca's head and wounded him. The delinquent, who was a stranger to the district, was seized and tortured to confess who had ordered him to do it. He stated that all the Sinchis of Cuyo-suyu, who were Cuyo Ccapac, Ayan-quilalama, and Apu Cunaraqui, had conspired to kill the Inca and rebel. This was false, for it had been extorted from fear of the torture or, as some say, he said it because he belonged to a hostile tribe and wished to do them harm. But the Inca, having heard what the potter said, ordered all the Sinchis to be killed with great cruelty. After their deaths he slaughtered the people, leaving none alive except some children and old women. Thus was that nation destroyed, and its towns are desolate to this day.

XXXV. THE OTHER NATIONS CONQUERED BY INCA YUPANQUI, EITHER IN PERSON OR THROUGH HIS BROTHER INCA ROCCA.

Inca Yupanqui and his brother Inca Rocca, who was very cruel, had determined to oppress and subdue all the nations who wished to be independent and would not submit to them. They knew that there were two Sinchis in a town called Ollantay-tampu, six leagues from Cuzco, the one named Paucar-Ancho and the other Tocori Tupac, who ruled over the Ollantay-tampus, but would not come to do homage, nor did their people wish to do so. The Inca marched against them with a large army and gave them battle. Inca Rocca was severely wounded, but at last the Ollantay-tampus were conquered. [All were killed, the place was destroyed so that no memory was left of it][89] and the Inca returned to Cuzco.

[Note 89: This is untrue. The splendid ruins remain to this day. The place was long held against the Spaniards by Inca Manco.]

There was another Sinchi named Illacumpi, chief of two towns four leagues from Cuzco, called Cugma and Huata. Inca Yupanqui and Inca Rocca sent to him to do homage, but he replied that he was as good as they were and free, and that if they wanted anything, they must get it with their lances. For this answer the Inca made war upon the said Sinchi. He united his forces with those of two other Sinchis, his companions, named Paucar Tupac and Puma Lloqui, and went forth to fight the Inca. But they were defeated and killed, with nearly all their people. The Inca desolated that town with fire and sword, and with very great cruelty. He then returned to Cuzco and triumphed for that victory.

The Inca received information, after this, that there was a town called Huancara, 11 leagues from Cuzco, ruled by Sinchis named Ascascahuana and Urcu-cuna. So a message was sent to them, calling upon them to give reverence and obedience to the Inca and to pay tribute. They replied that they were not women to come and serve, that they were in their native place, and that if any one came to seek their lands, they would defend themselves. Moved to anger by this reply, Inca Yupanqui and Inca Rocca made war, killed the Sinchis and most of their people and brought the rest prisoners to Cuzco, to force them into obedience.

Next they marched to another town called Toguaro, six leagues from Huancara, killing the Sinchi, named Alca-parihuana, and all the people, not sparing any but the children, that they might grow and repeople that land. With similar cruelties in all the towns, the Inca reduced to pay tribute the Cotabambas, Cotaneras, Umasayus, and Aymaracs, being the principal provinces of Cunti-suyu.

The Inca then attacked the province of the Soras, 40 leagues from Cuzco. The natives came forth to resist, asking why the invaders sought their lands, telling them to depart or they would be driven out by force. Over this question there was a battle, and two towns of the Soras were subdued at that time, the one called Chalco, the other Soras. The Sinchi of Chalco was named Chalco-pusaycu, that of Soras Huacralla. They were taken prisoners to Cuzco, and there was a triumph over them.

There was another place called Acos, 10 or 11 leagues from Cuzco. The two Sinchis of it were named Ocacique and Utu-huasi. These were strongly opposed to the demands of the Inca and made a very strenuous resistance. The Inca marched against them with a great army. But he met with serious difficulty in this conquest, for the Acos defended themselves most bravely and wounded Pachacuti on the head with a stone. He would not desist, but it was not until after a long time that they were conquered. He killed nearly all the natives of Acos, and those who were pardoned and survived after that cruel slaughter, were banished to the neighbourhood of Huamanca, to a place now called Acos[90].

[Note 90: Acobamba, the present capital of the province of Angaraes.]

In all these campaigns which have been described, Inca Rocca was the companion in arms, and participator in the triumphs of Inca Yupanqui. It is to be noted that in all the subdued provinces chiefs were placed, superseding or killing the native Sinchis. Those who were appointed, acted as guards or captains of the conquered places, holding office in the Inca's name and during his pleasure. In this way the conquered provinces were oppressed and tyrannized over by the yoke of servitude. A superior was appointed over all the others who were nominated to each town, as general or governor. In their language this officer was called Tucuyrico[91], which means "he who knows and oversees all."

[Note 91: Tucuyricuc, he who sees all. Tucuy means all. Ricini to see. Garcilasso de la Vega, I. lib. ii. cap. 14. Balboa, p. 115. Montesinos, p. 55. Santillana, p. 17.]

Thus in the first campaign undertaken by Pachacuti Inca Yupanqui, after the defeat of the Chancas, he subdued the country as far as the Soras, 40 leagues to the west of Cuzco. The other nations, and some in Cunti-suyu, from fear at seeing the cruelties committed on the conquered, came in to submit, to avoid destruction. [But they ever submitted against their wills.]

XXXVI. PACHACUTI INCA YUPANQUI ENDOWS THE HOUSE OF THE SUN WITH GREAT WEALTH.

After Pachacuti Inca Yupanqui had conquered the lands and nations mentioned above, and had triumphed over them, he came to visit the House of the Sun and the Mama-cunas or nuns who were there. He assisted one day, to see how the Mama-cunas served the dinner of the Sun. This was to offer much richly cooked food to the image or idol of the Sun, and then to put it into a great fire on an altar. The same order was taken with the liquor. The chief of the Mama-cunas saluted the Sun with a small vase, and the rest was thrown on the fire. Besides this many jars full of that liquor were poured into a trough which had a drain, all being offerings to the Sun. This service was performed with vessels of clay. As Pachacuti considered that the material of the vases was too poor, he presented very complete sets of vases of gold and silver for all the service that was necessary. To adorn the house more richly he caused a plate of fine gold to be made, two palmas broad and the length of the court-yard. He ordered this to be nailed high up on the wall in the manner of a cornice, passing all round the court-yard. This border or cornice of gold remained there down to the time of the Spaniards.

XXXVII. PACHACUTI INCA YUPANQUI CONQUERS THE PROVINCE OF COLLA-SUYU.

To the south of Cuzco there was a province called Colla-suyu or Collao, consisting of plain country, which was very populous. At the time that Pachacuti Inca Yupanqui was at Cuzco after having conquered the provinces already mentioned, the Sinchi of Collao was named Chuchi Ccapac or Colla Ccapac, which is all one. This Chuchi Ccapac increased so much in power and wealth among those nations of Colla-suyu, that he was respected by all the Collas, who called him Inca Ccapac.

Pachacuti Inca Yupanqui determined to conquer him from a motive of jealousy, together with all the provinces of the Collao. With this object he assembled his army and marched on the route to the Collao in order to attack Chuchi Ccapac who waited for him at Hatun-Colla, a town of the Collao where he resided, 40 leagues from Cuzco, without having taken further notice of the coming nor of the forces of Inca Yupanqui. When he came near to Hatun Colla, the Inca sent a message to Chuchi Colla, requesting him to serve and obey him or else to prepare for battle, when they would try their fortunes. This message caused much heaviness to Chuchi Colla, but he replied proudly that he waited for the Inca to come and do homage to him like the other nations that had been conquered by him, and that if the Inca did not choose to do so, he would prepare his head, with which he intended to drink in his triumph after the victory which he would win if they should come to a battle.

After this reply Inca Yupanqui ordered his army to approach that of Chuchi Ccapac the next day, which was drawn up ready to fight. Soon after they came in sight, the two forces attacked each other, and the battle continued for a long time without either side gaining any advantage. Inca Yupanqui, who was very dexterous in fighting, was assisting in every part, giving orders, combating, and animating his troops. Seeing that the Collas resisted so resolutely, and stood so firmly in the battle, he turned his face to his men saying in a loud voice: "O Incas of Cuzco! conquerors of all the land! Are you not ashamed that people so inferior to you, and unequal in weapons, should be equal to you and resist for so long a time?" With this he returned to the fight, and the troops, touched by this rebuke, pressed upon their enemies in such sort that they were broken and defeated. Inca Yupanqui, being an experienced warrior, knew that the completion of the victory consisted in the capture of Chuchi Ccapac. Although he was fighting, he looked out for his enemy in all directions and, seeing him in the midst of his people, the Inca attacked them at the head of his guards, took him prisoner, and delivered him to a soldier with orders to take him to the camp and keep him safe. The Inca and his army then completed the victory and engaged in the pursuit, until all the Sinchis and captains that could be found were captured. Pachacuti went to Hatun-colla, the residence and seat of government of Chuchi Ccapac, where he remained until all the provinces which obeyed Chuchi Ccapac, were reduced to obedience, and brought many rich presents of gold, silver, cloths, and other precious things.

Leaving a garrison and a governor in the Collao to rule in his name, the Inca returned to Cuzco, taking Chuchi Ccapac as a prisoner with the others. He entered Cuzco, where a solemn triumph was prepared. Chuchi Colla and the other Colla prisoners were placed before the Inca's litter dressed in long robes covered with tassels in derision and that they might be known. Having arrived at the House of the Sun, the captives and spoils were offered to the image of the Sun, and the Inca, or the priest for him, trod on all the spoils and captives that Pachacuti had taken in the Collao, which was great honour to the Inca. When the triumph was over, to give it a good finish, the Inca caused the head of Chuchi Ccapac to be cut off, and put in the house called Llasa-huasi[92], with those of the other Sinchis he had killed. He caused the other Sinchis and captains of Chuchi Ccapac to be given to the wild beasts, kept shut up for the purpose, in a house called Samca-huasi[93].

[Note 92: Llasa-huasi. Llasa means weight, from llasani to weigh. Huasi a house.]

[Note 93: Samgaguacy. This should be Samca-huasi, a prison for grave offences. Serpents and toads were put into the prison with the delinquents. Mossi, p. 233.]

In these conquests Pachacuti was very cruel to the vanquished, and people were so terrified at the cruelties that they submitted and obeyed from fear of being made food for wild beasts, or burnt, or otherwise cruelly tormented rather than resist in arms. It was thus with the people of Cunti-suyu who, seeing the cruelty and power of Inca Yupanqui, humiliated themselves and promised obedience. It was for the cause and reason stated, and because they were threatened with destruction if they did not come to serve and obey.

Chuchi Ccapac had subjugated a region more than 160 leagues from north to south, over which he was Sinchi or, as he called himself, Ccapac or Colla-Ccapac, from within 20 leagues of Cuzco as far as the Chichas, with all the bounds of Arequipa and the sea-coast to Atacama, and the forests of the Musus. For at this time, seeing the violence and power with which the Inca of Cuzco came down upon those who opposed him, without pardoning anyone, many Sinchis followed his example, and wanted to do the same in other parts, where each one lived, so that all was confusion and tyranny in this kingdom, no one being secure of his own property. We shall relate in their places, as the occasion offers, the stories of the Sinchis, tyrants, besides those of the Incas who, from the time of Inca Yupanqui, began to get provinces into their power, and tyrannize over the inhabitants.

Inca Yupanqui, as has already been narrated, had given the House of the Sun all things necessary for its services, besides which, after he came from Colla-suyu, he presented many things brought from there for the image of the Sun, and for the mummies of his ancestors which were kept in the House of the Sun. He also gave them servants and lands. He ordered that the huacas of Cuzco should be adopted and venerated in all the conquered provinces, ordaining new ceremonies for their worship and abolishing the ancient rites. He charged his eldest legitimate son, named Amaru Tupac Inca, with the duty of abolishing the huacas which were not held to be legitimate, and to see that the others were maintained and received the sacrifices ordered by the Inca. Huayna Yamqui Yupanqui, another son of Inca Yupanqui, was associated with the heir in this duty.

XXXVIII.PACHACUTI INCA YUPANQUI SENDS AN ARMY TO CONQUER THE PROVINCE OF CHINCHAY-SUYU.

When Pachacuti Inca Yupanqui returned from the conquest of Colla-suyu and the neighbouring provinces, as has been narrated in the preceding chapter, he was well stricken in years, though not tired of wars, nor was his thirst for dominion satisfied. Owing to his age he chose to remain at Cuzco, as the seat of his government, to establish the lands he had subdued, in the way which he well knew how to establish. In order to lose no time in extending his conquests, he assembled his people, from among whom he chose 70,000 provided with arms and all things necessary for a military campaign. He nominated his brother, Ccapac Yupanqui, to be Captain-General, giving him for colleagues another of his brothers named Huayna Yupanqui, and one of his sons named Apu Yamqui Yupanqui. Among the other special captains in this army was one named Anco Ayllo of the Chanca nation, who had remained a prisoner in Cuzco from the time that the Inca conquered the Chanca's at Cuzco and at Ichu-pampa. He had ever since been sad and brooding, thinking of a way of escape. But he dissimulated so well that the Inca treated him as a brother and trusted him. Hence the Inca nominated him as commander of all the Chancas in the army. For each nation the Inca gave a captain from among their own people, because he would understand how to rule them and they would obey him better. This Anco Ayllo, seeing there was an opportunity for fulfilling his desire, showed satisfaction at receiving this commission from the Inca, and promised to do valuable service, as he knew those nations whose conquest was about to be undertaken. When the army was ready to march, the Inca gave the Captain-General his own arms of gold, and to the other captains he gave arms with which to enter the battles. He made a speech to them, exhorting them to achieve success, showing them the honourable reward they would obtain, and the favours he, as a friend, would show them, if they served in that war. He gave special orders to Ccapac Yupanqui that he should advance with his conquering army as far as a province called Yana-mayu, the boundary of the nation of the Hatun-huayllas, and that there he should set up the Inca's boundary pillars, and he was on no account to advance further. He was to conquer up to that point and then return to Cuzco, leaving sufficient garrisons in the subjugated lands. He was also to establish posts at every half league, which they call chasquis, by means of which the Inca would be daily informed of what had happened and was being done[94].

[Note 94: For accounts of the chasquis or Inca couriers see Garcilasso de la Vega, ii. pp. 49, 60, 119, 120, 121. Balboa, p. 248.

Polo de Ondegardo, p. 169.]

Ccapac Yupanqui set out from Cuzco with these orders, and desolated all the provinces which did not submit. On arriving at a fortress called Urco-collac, near Parcos, in the country of Huamanca, he met with valorous resistance from the inhabitants. Finally he conquered them. In the battle the Chancas distinguished themselves so that they gained more honour than the Cuzcos orejones and the other nations.

This news came to the Inca, who was much annoyed that the Chancas should have distinguished themselves more, and had gained more honour than the Incas. He imagined that it would make them proud, so he proposed to have them killed. He sent a messenger ordering Ccapac Yupanqui to lay a plan for killing all the Chancas in the best way he could devise, and if he did not kill them, the Inca would kill him. The runner of the Inca reached Ccapac Yupanqui with this order, but it could not be kept a secret. It became known to a wife of Ccapac Yupanqui, who was a sister of Anco Ayllo, the captain of the Chancas. This woman told her brother, who always longed for his liberty, and now was urgently minded to save his life. He secretly addressed his Chanca soldiers, putting before them the cruel order of the Inca, and the acquisition of their liberty if they would follow him. They all agreed to his proposal. When they came to Huarac-tambo, in the neighbourhood of the city of Huanuco, all the Chancas fled with their captain Anco Ayllo, and besides the Chancas other tribes followed this chief. Passing by the province of Huayllas they pillaged it, and, continuing their route in flight from the Incas, they agreed to seek a rugged and mountainous land where the Incas, even if they sought them, would not be able to find them. So they entered the forests between Chachapoyas and Huanuco, and went on to the province of Ruparupa. These are the people who are settled on the river Pacay and, according to the received report, thence to the eastward by the river called Cocama which falls into the great river Marañon. They were met with by the captain Gomez d'Arias, who entered by Huanuco, in the time of the Marquis of Cañete, in the year 1556. Though Ccapac Yupanqui went in chase of the Chancas, they were so rapid in their flight that he was unable to overtake them[95].

[Note 95: Garcilasso de la Vega also gives an account of the flight of the Chancas under Anco-ayllu or Hanco-hualla, ii. pp. 82, 329.]

In going after them Ccapac Yupanqui went as far as Caxamarca, beyond the line he was ordered not to pass by the Inca. Although he had the order in his mind, yet when he saw that province of Caxamarca, how populous it was and rich in gold and silver, by reason of the great Sinchi, named Gusmanco Ccapac, who ruled there and was a great tyrant, having robbed many provinces round Caxamarca, Ccapac Yupanqui resolved to conquer it, although he had no commission from his brother for undertaking such an enterprise. On commencing to enter the land of Caxamarca, it became known to Gusmanco Ccapac. That chief summoned his people, and called upon another Sinchi, his tributary, named Chimu Ccapac, chief of the territory where now stands the city of Truxillo on the coast of Peru. Their combined forces marched against Ccapac Yupanqui, who by a certain ambush, and other stratagems, defeated, routed and captured the two Sinchis Gusmanco Ccapac and Chimu Ccapac, taking vast treasure of gold, silver and other precious things, such as gems, and coloured shells, which these natives value more than silver or gold.

Ccapac Yupanqui collected all the treasure in the square of Caxamarca, where he then was; and when he saw such immense wealth he became proud and vainglorious, saying that he had gained and acquired more than his brother the Inca. His arrogance and boasting came to the ears of his sovereign, who, although he felt it deeply and desired an opportunity to kill him, dissimulated for a time and waited until the return to Cuzco. Inca Yupanqui feared that his brother would rebel, and for this reason he appeared to be pleased before the envoys sent by Ccapac Yupanqui. He sent them back with orders that Ccapac Yupanqui should return to Cuzco with the treasure that had been taken in the war, as well as the principal men of the subdued provinces, and the sons of Gusmanco Ccapac and Chimu Ccapac. The great chiefs themselves were to remain, in their territories with a sufficient garrison to keep those lands obedient to the Inca. On receiving this order Ccapac Yupanqui set out for Cuzco with all the treasure, and marched to the capital full of pride and arrogance. Inca Yupanqui, who himself subdued so many lands and gained so much honour, became jealous, as some say afraid, and sought excuses for killing his brother. When he knew that Ccapac Yupanqui had reached Limatambo, eight leagues from Cuzco, he ordered his lieutenant-governor named Inca Capon, to go there and cut off the head of Ccapac Yupanqui. The reasons given were that he had allowed Anco Ayllo to escape, and had gone beyond the line prescribed. The governor went and, in obedience to his orders, he killed the Inca's two brothers Ccapac Yupanqui and Huayna Yupanqui. The Inca ordered the rest to enter Cuzco, triumphing over their victories. This was done, the Inca treading on the spoils, and granting rewards. They say that he regretted that his brother had gained so much honour, and that he wished that he had sent his son who was to be his successor, named Tupac Inca Yupanqui, that he might have enjoyed such honour, and that this jealousy led him to kill his brother.

XXXIX. PACHACUTI INCA YUPANQUI PLANTS MITIMAES IN ALL THE LANDS HE HAD CONQUERED.

As all the conquests made by this Inca were attended with such violence and cruelties, with such spoliation and force, and the people who became his subjects by acquisition, or to speak more correctly by rapine, were numerous, they obeyed so long as they felt the force compelling them, and, as soon as they were a little free from that fear, they presently rebelled and resumed their liberty. Then the Inca was obliged to conquer them again. Turning many things in his mind, and seeking for remedies, how he could settle once for all the numerous provinces he had conquered, at last he hit upon a plan which, although adapted to the object he sought to attain, and coloured with some appearance of generosity, was really the worst tyranny he perpetrated. He ordered visitors to go through all the subdued provinces, with orders to measure and survey them, and to bring him models of the natural features in clay. This was done. The models and reports were brought before the Inca. He examined them and considered the mountainous fastnesses and the plains. He ordered the visitors to look well to what he would do. He then began to demolish the fastnesses and to have their inhabitants moved to plain country, and those of the plains were moved to mountainous regions, so far from each other, and each so far from their native country, that they could not return to it. Next the Inca ordered the visitors to go and do with the people what they had seen him do with the models. They went and did so.

He gave orders to others to go to the same districts, and, jointly with the tucuricos, to take some young men, with their wives, from each district. This was done and they were brought to Cuzco from all the provinces, from one 30, from another 100, more or less according to the population of each district. These selected people were presented before the Inca, who ordered that they should be taken to people various parts. Those of Chinchay-suyu were sent to Anti-suyu, those of Cunti-suyu to Colla-suyu, so far from their native country that they could not communicate with their relations or countrymen. He ordered that they should be settled in valleys similar to those in their native land, and that they should have seeds from those lands that they might be preserved and not perish, giving them land to sow without stint, and removing the natives.

The Incas called these colonists mitimaes[96], which means "transported" or "moved," He ordered them to learn the language of the country to which they were removed, but not to forget the general language, which was the Quichua, and which he had ordered that all his subjects in all the conquered provinces must learn and know. With it conversation and business could be carried on, for it was the clearest and richest of the dialects. The Inca gave the colonists authority and power to enter the houses of the natives at all hours, night or day, to see what they said, did or arranged, with orders to report all to the nearest governor, so that it might be known if anything was plotted against the government of the Inca, who, knowing the evil he had done, feared all in general, and knew that no one served him voluntarily, but only by force. Besides this the Inca put garrisons into all the fortresses of importance, composed of natives of Cuzco or the neighbourhood, which garrisons were called michecrima[97].

[Note 96: The system of mitimaes was a very important part of the Inca polity. It is frequently referred to by Cieza de Leon, and described by Garcilasso de la Vega, ii. p. 215. See also Balboa, pp. 28, 114,143,249. Molina, pp. 4, 22, 23. Yamqui Pachacuti, pp. 95, 97, Polo de Ondegardo, p. 161.]

[Note 97: Michec a shepherd, hence a governor. Rimay to speak.]

XL. THE COLLAS, SONS OF CHUCHI CCAPAC, REBEL AGAINST INCA YUPANQUI TO OBTAIN THEIR FREEDOM.

After Inca Yupanqui had celebrated the triumphs and festivities consequent on the conquest of Chinchay-suyu, and arranged the system of mitimaes, he dismissed the troops. He himself went to Yucay, where he built the edifices, the ruins of which may still be seen. These being finished, he went down the valley of Yucay to a place which is now called Tambo, eight leagues from Cuzco, where he erected some magnificent buildings. The sons of Chuchi Ccapac, the great Sinchi of the Collao, had to labour as captives at the masonry and other work. Their father, as has already been narrated, was conquered in the Collao and killed by the Inca. These sons of Chuchi Ccapac, feeling that they were being vilely treated, and remembering that they were the sons of so great a man as their father, also seeing that the Inca had disbanded his army, agreed to risk their lives in obtaining their freedom. One night they fled, with all the people who were there, and made such speed that, although the Inca sent after them, they could not be overtaken. Along the route they took, they kept raising the inhabitants against the Inca. Much persuasion was not needed, because, as they were obeying by force, they only sought the first opportunity to rise. On this favourable chance, many nations readily rebelled, even those who were very near Cuzco, but principally the Collao and all its provinces.

The Inca, seeing this, ordered a great army to be assembled, and sought the favour of auxiliaries from Gusmanco Ccapac and Chimu Ccapac. He collected a great number of men, made sacrifices calpa[98], and buried some children alive, which is called capa cocha, to induce their idols to favour them in that war. All being ready, the Inca nominated two of his sons as captains of the army, valorous men, named the one Tupac Ayar Manco, the other Apu Paucar Usnu. The Inca left Cuzco with more than 200,000 warriors, and marched against the sons of Chuchi Ccapac, who also had a great power of men and arms, and were anxious to meet the Incas and fight for their lives against the men of Cuzco.

[Note 98: Calpa means force, vigour; also an army.]

As both were seeking each other, they soon met, and joined in a stubborn and bloody battle, in which there was great slaughter, because one side fought for life and liberty and the other for honour. As those of Cuzco were better disciplined and drilled, and more numerous than their adversaries, they had the advantage. But the Collas preferred to die fighting rather than to become captives to one so cruel and inhuman as the Inca. So they opposed themselves to the arms of the orejones, who, with great cruelties, killed as many of the Collas as opposed their advance. The sons of the Inca did great things in the battle, with their own hands, on that day. The Collas were defeated, most of them being killed or taken prisoners. Those who fled were followed to a place called Lampa. There the wounded were cared for, and the squadrons refreshed. The Inca ordered his two sons, Tupac Ayar Manco and Apu Paucar Usnu, to press onward, conquering the country as far as the Chichas, where they were to set up their cairns and return. The Inca then returned to Cuzco, for a triumph over the victory he had gained.

The Inca arrived at Cuzco, triumphed and celebrated the victory with festivities. And because he found that a son had been born to him, he raised him before the Sun, offered him, and gave him the name of Tupac Inca Yupanqui. In his name he offered treasures of gold and silver to the Sun, and to the other oracles and huacas, and also made the sacrifice of capa cocha. Besides this he made the most solemn and costly festivals that had ever been known, throughout the land. This was done because Inca Yupanqui wished that this Tupac Inca should succeed him, although he had other older and legitimate sons by his wife and sister Mama Anahuarqui. For, although the custom of these tyrants was that the eldest legitimate son should succeed, it was seldom observed, the Inca preferring the one he liked best, or whose mother he loved most, or he who was the ablest among the brothers.

XLI.AMARU TUPAC INCA AND APU PAUCAR USNU CONTINUE THE CONQUEST OF THE COLLAO AND AGAIN SUBDUE THE COLLAS.

As soon as the Inca returned to Cuzco, leaving his two sons Tupac Amaru and Apu Paucar Usnu[99] in the Callao, those captains set out from Lampa, advancing to Hatun-Colla, where they knew that the Collas had rallied their troops to fight the Cuzcos once more, and that they had raised one of the sons of Chuchi Ccapac to be Inca. The Incas came to the place where the Collas were awaiting them in arms. They met and fought valorously, many being killed on both sides. At the end of the battle the Collas were defeated and their new Inca was taken prisoner. Thus for a third time were the Collas conquered by the Cuzcos. By order of the Inca, his sons, generals of the war, left the new Inca of the Collas at Hatun-Colla, as a prisoner well guarded and re-captured. The other captains went on, continuing their conquests, as the Inca had ordered, to the confines of Charcas and the Chichas.

[Note 99: Tupac Amaru. Tupac means royal, and amaru a serpent. Apu a chief, paucar beautiful and usnu a judgment seat.]

While his sons prosecuted the war, Pachacuti their father, finished the edifices at Tambo, and constructed the ponds and pleasure houses of Yucay. He erected, on a hill near Cuzco, called Patallata, some sumptuous houses, and many others in the neighbourhood of the capital. He also made many channels of water both for use and for pleasure; and ordered all the governors of provinces who were under his sway, to build pleasure houses on the most convenient sites, ready for him when he should visit their commands.

While Inca Yupanqui proceeded with these measures, his sons had completed the conquest of the Collao. When they arrived in the vicinity of Charcas, the natives of Paria, Tapacari, Cochabambas, Poconas and Charcas retreated to the country of the Chichas and Chuyes, in order to make a combined resistance to the Incas, who arrived where their adversaries were assembled, awaiting the attack. The Inca army was in three divisions. A squadron of 5000 men went by the mountains, another of 20,000 by the side of the sea, and the rest by the direct road. They arrived at the strong position held by the Charcas and their allies, and fought with them. The Incas were victorious, and took great spoils of silver extracted by those natives from the mines of Porco. It is to be noted that nothing was ever known of the 5000 orejones who entered by the mountains or what became of them. Leaving all these provinces conquered, and subdued, Amaru Tupac Inca and Apu Paucar Usnu returned to Cuzco where they triumphed over their victories, Pachacuti granting them many favours, and rejoicing with many festivals and sacrifices to idols.

XLII.PACHACUTI INCA YUPANQUI NOMINATES HIS SON TUPAC INCA YUPANQUI AS HIS SUCCESSOR.

Pachacuti Inca Yupanqui was now very old; and he determined to nominate a successor to take his place after his death. He called together the Incas his relations, of the ayllus of Hanan-cuzco and Hurin-cuzco and said, "My friends and relations! I am now, as you see, very old, and I desire to leave you, when my days are over, one who will govern and defend you from your enemies. Some propose that I should name Amaru Tupac Inca, but it does not appear to me that he has the qualifications to govern so great a lordship as that which I have acquired. I, therefore, desire to nominate another with whom you will be more content." The relations, in their reply, gave thanks to the Inca, and declared that they would derive great benefit from his nomination. He then said that he named his son Tupac Inca, and ordered him to come forth from the house. He had been there for 15 or 16 years to be brought up, without any one seeing him except very rarely and as a great favour. He was now shown to the people, and the Inca presently ordered a fringe of gold to be placed in the hand of the image of the Sun, with the head-dress called pillaca-llaytu[100]. After Tupac Inca had made his obeisance to his father, the Inca and the rest rose and went before the image of the Sun where they made their sacrifices and offered capa cocha to that deity. Then they offered the new Inca Tupac Yupanqui, beseeching the Sun to protect and foster him, and to make him so that all should hold and judge him to be a child of the Sun and father of his people. This done the oldest and principal orejones took Tupac Inca to the Sun, and the priests took the fringe from the hands of the image, which they call mascapaycha, and placed it over the head of Tupac Inca Yupanqui until it rested on his forehead. He was declared Inca Ccapac and seated in front of the Sun on a seat of gold, called duho[101], garnished with emeralds and other precious stones. Seated there, they clothed him in the ccapac hongo[102], placed the suntur paucar in his hand, gave him the other insignia of Inca, and the priests raised him on their shoulders. When these ceremonies were completed, Pachacuti Inca Yupanqui ordered that his son Tupac Inca should remain shut up in the House of the Sun, performing the fasts which it is the custom to go through before receiving the order of chivalry; which ceremony consisted in opening the ears. The Inca ordered that what had been done should not be made public until he gave the command to publish it.
[Note 100: Pillaca-llatu is a cloth or cloak woven of two colours, black and brown.]
[Note 101: This word is corrupt. Tiana is the word for a seat.]
[Note 102: Ccapac uncu. The word uncu means a tunic.]

XLIII.HOW PACHACUTI ARMED HIS SON TUPAC INCA.

Pachacuti Inca Yupanqui found happiness in leaving memory of himself. With this object he did extraordinary things as compared with those of his ancestors, in building edifices, celebrating triumphs, not allowing himself to be seen except as a great favour shown to the people, for as such it was considered, on the day that he appeared. Then he ordered that no one should come to behold him without worshipping and bringing something in his hand to offer him. This custom was continued by all his descendants, and was observed inviolably. [Thus, from the time of this Pachacuti began an unheard of and inhuman tyranny in addition to the tyrannies of his ancestors.] As he was now old and desirous of perpetuating his name, it appeared to him that he would obtain his desire by giving authority to his son and successor named Tupac Inca. So the boy was brought up, confined in the House of the Sun for more than 16 years, seeing no one but his tutors and masters until he was brought and presented to the Sun, to be nominated as has already been explained. To invest him at the huarachico the Inca ordered a new way of giving the order of chivalry. For this he built round the city four other houses for prayer to the Sun, with much apparatus of gold idols, huacas and service, for his son to perambulate these stations after he had been armed as a knight.

Affairs being in this state, there came to the Inca Pachacuti, his son Amaru Tupac Inca, who had been named by his father as his successor some years before, because he was the eldest legitimate son. He said, "Father Inca! I understand that you have a son in the House of the Sun whom you have ordered to be successor after your own days. Order that he may be show to me." The Inca, looking upon this as boldness on the part of Amaru Tupac, replied, "It is true, and I desire you and your wife shall be his vassals, and that you shall serve and obey him as your Lord and Inca." Amaru replied that he wished to do so, and that for this reason, he desired to see him and offer sacrifice to him, and that orders should be given to take him where his brother was. The Inca gave permission for this, Amaru Tupac Inca taking what was necessary for the ceremony, and being brought to where Tupac Inca was fasting. When Amaru saw him in such majesty of wealth and surroundings, he fell on his face to the earth, adoring, offering sacrifices and obedience. On learning that it was his brother, Tupac Inca raised him and saluted him in the face. Presently Inca Yupanqui caused the necessary preparations to be made for investing his son with the order of chivalry. When all was ready, the Inca, accompanied by all his principal relations and courtiers, went to the House of the Sun, where they brought out Tupac Inca with great solemnity and pomp. For they carried with him all the idols of the Sun, Vircocha, the other huacas, moro-urco. All being placed in order with such pomp as had never been seen before, they all went to the great square of the city, in the centre of which a bonfire was made. All relations and friends then killed many animals, offering them as sacrifices by throwing them into the flames. They worshipped the heir, offering him rich gifts, the first that brought a gift being his father. Following the example all the rest adored, seeing that his father had shown him reverence. Thus did the orejones Incas and all the rest who were present, seeing that for this they had been called and invited, to bring their gifts and offer them to their new Inca.

This being done, the festival called Ccapac Raymi was commenced, being the feast of kings, and consequently the most solemn festival kept by these people. When the ceremonies had been performed, they bored the ears of Tupac Inca Yupanqui, which is their mode of investiture into the order of chivalry and nobility. He was then taken to the stations of the Houses of the Sun, giving him the weapons and other insignia of war. This being finished his father the Inca Yupanqui gave him, for his wife, one of his sisters named Mama Ocllo, who was a very beautiful woman with much ability and wisdom.

XLIV. PACHACUTI INCA YUPANQUI SENDS HIS SON TUPAC INCA

YUPANQUI TO CONQUER CHINCHAY-SUYU.

The Inca Yupanqui desired that his son should be employed on some service that would bring him fame, as soon as he had been proclaimed his successor, and armed as a knight. He had information that Chinchay-suyu was a region where name and treasure might be acquired, especially from a Sinchi named Chuqui-Sota in Chachapoyas. He, therefore, ordered all preparations to be made for the conquest of Chinchay-suyu. He gave the prince for his tutors, captains, and captains-general of his army, two of his brothers, the one named Auqui Yupanqui and the other Tilca Yupanqui. The army being assembled and the preparations made, they set out from Cuzco.

Tupac went in such pomp and majesty that, where he passed, no one dared to look him in the face, in such veneration was he held. The people left the roads along which he had to pass and, ascending the hills on either side, worshipped and adored. They pulled out their eyebrows and eyelashes, and blowing on them, they made offering to the Inca. Others offered handfuls of a very precious herb called coca. When he arrived at the villages, he put on the dress and head-gear of that district, for all were different in their dress and head-gear as they are now. For Inca Yupanqui, so as to know each nation he had conquered, ordered that each one should have a special dress and head-gear, which they call pillu, llaytu and chuco, different one from the other, so as to be easily distinguished and recognized. Seating himself, Tupac Inca made a solemn sacrifice of animals and birds, burning them in a fire which was kindled in his presence; and in this way they worshipped the sun, which they believed to be God.

In this manner Tupac Inca began to repeat the conquests and tyranny of all his ancestors and his father. For, although many nations were conquered by his father, almost all were again with arms in their hands to regain their liberty, and the rest to defend themselves. As Tupac Inca advanced with such power, force and pride, he not only claimed the subjection of the people, but also usurped the veneration they gave to their gods or devils, for truly he and his father made them worship all with more veneration than the Sun.

Tupac Inca finally marched out of Cuzco and began to proceed with measures for subduing the people in the near vicinity. In the province of the Quichuas[103] he conquered and occupied the fortresses of Tohara, Cayara, and Curamba, and in the province of Angaraes the fortresses of Urco-colla and Huaylla-pucara, taking its Sinchi named Chuquis Huaman prisoner. In the province of Xauxa he took Sisiquilla Pucara, and in the province of Huayllas the fortresses of Chuncu-marca and Pillahua-marca. In Chachapoyas the fortress of Piajajalca fell before him, and he took prisoner a very rich chief named Chuqui Sota. He conquered the province of the Paltas, and the valleys of Pacasmayu and Chimu, which is now Truxillo. He destroyed it as Chimu Ccapac had been subdued before. He also conquered the province of the Cañaris, and those who resisted were totally destroyed. The Cañaris submitted from fear, and he took their Sinchis, named Pisar Ccapac, Cañar Ccapac and Chica Ccapac, and built an impregnable fortress there called Quinchi-caxa.

[Note 103: The province of the Quichuas was in the valley of the Pachachaca, above Abancay.]

Tupac Inca Yupanqui then returned to Cuzco with much treasure and many prisoners. He was well received by his father with a most sumptuous triumph, and with the applause of all the orejones of Cuzco. They had many feasts and sacrifices, and to please the people they celebrated the festival called Inti Raymi with feasts and dances, a time of great rejoicing. The Inca granted many favours for the sake of his son Tupac Inca, that he might have the support of his subjects, which was what he desired. For as he was very old and unable to move about, feeling the approach of death, his aim was to leave his son in the possession of the confidence of his army.

XLV.HOW PACHACUTI INCA YUPANQUI VISITED THE PROVINCES CONQUERED FOR HIM BY HIS CAPTAINS.

It has been related how the Inca Yupanqui placed garrisons of Cuzco soldiers, and a governor called tucuyrico in all the provinces he conquered and oppressed. It must be known that owing to his absorbing occupations in conquering other provinces, training warriors, and placing his son in command for the conquest of Chinchay-suyu, he had not been able to put his final intentions and will into execution, which was to make those he oppressed submissive subjects and tributaries. Seeing that the people were in greater fear at beholding the valour of Tupac Inca, he determined to have a visitation of the land, and nominated 16 visitors, four for each of the four suyus or divisions of the empire, which are Cunti-suyu from Cuzco south and west as far as the South Sea, Chinchay-suyu from Cuzco to the north and west, Anti-suyu from Cuzco to the east, and Colla-suyu from Cuzco to the south, south-west, and south-east.

These visitors each went to the part to which he was appointed, and inspected, before all things, the work of the tucuyricos and the methods of their government. They caused irrigating channels to be constructed for the crops, broke up land where this had been neglected, built andenes or cultivated terraces, and took up pastures for the Sun, the Inca, and Cuzco. Above all they imposed very heavy tribute on all the produce, [so that they all went about to rob and desolate property and persons]. The visitations occupied two years. When they were completed the visitors returned to Cuzco, bringing with them certain cloths descriptive of the provinces they had visited. They reported fully to the Inca all that they had found and done.

Besides these, the Inca also despatched other orejones as overseers to make roads and hospices on the routes of the Inca, ready for the use of his soldiers. These overseers set out, and made roads, now called "of the Inca," over the mountains and along the sea coast. Those on the sea coast are all provided, at the sides, with high walls of adobe, wherever it was possible to build them, except in the deserts where there are no building materials. These roads go from Quito to Chile, and into the forests of the Andes. Although the Inca did not complete all, suffice it that he made a great part of the roads, which were finished by his sons and grandsons.

XLVI.TUPAC INCA YUPANQUI SETS OUT, A SECOND TIME, BY ORDER OF HIS FATHER, TO CONQUER WHAT REMAINED UNSUBDUED IN CHINCHAY-SUYU.

Pachacuti Inca Yupanqui knew from the report made by his son when he returned from the conquest of Chinchay-suyu, that there were other great and rich nations and provinces beyond the furthest point reached by Tupac Inca. That no place might be left to conquer, the Inca ordered his son to return with a view to the subjugation of the parts of Quito. He assembled the troops and gave his son the same two brothers as his colleagues, Tilca Yupanqui and Anqui Yupanqui, who had gone with him on the former expedition. [Tupac inflicted unheard of cruelties and deaths on those who defended themselves and did not wish to give him obedience.]

In this way he arrived at Tumipampa, within the territory of Quito, whose Sinchi, named Pisar Ccapac, was confederated with Pilla-huaso, Sinchi of the provinces and site of Quito. These two chiefs had a great army and were determined to fight Tupac Inca for their country and lives. Tupac sent messengers to them, demanding that they should lay down their arms and give him obedience. They replied that they were in their own native country, that they were free, and did not wish to serve any one nor be tributaries.

Tupac and his colleagues rejoiced at this answer, because their wish was to find a pretext to encounter them with blows and to rob them, which was the principal object of the war. They say that the Inca army numbered more than 250,000 experienced soldiers. Tupac ordered them to march against the men of Quito and the Cañaris. They encountered each other, both sides fighting with resolution and skill. The victory was for a long time doubtful because the Quitos and Cañaris pressed stubbornly against their enemies. When the Inca saw this he got out of the litter in which he travelled, animated his people, and made signs for the 50,000 men who were kept in reserve for the last necessity. When these fresh troops appeared the Quitos and Cañaris were defeated and fled, the pursuit being continued with much bloodshed and cruelty, the victors shouting, "Ccapac Inca Yupanqui! Cuzco! Cuzco!" All the chiefs were killed. They captured Pilla-huaso in the vanguard. No quarter was given, in order to strike terror into those who heard of it.

Thence Inca Tupac marched to the place where now stands the city of San Francisco de Quito, where they halted to cure the wounded and give much needed rest to the others. So this great province remained subject, and Tupac sent a report of his proceedings to his father. Pachacuti rejoiced at the success of his son, and celebrated many festivals and sacrifices on receiving the tidings.

After Tupac Inca had rested at Cuzco, re-organized his army, and cured the wounded he went to Tumipampa, where his wife and sister bore him a son, to whom he gave the name of Titu Cusi Hualpa, afterwards known as Huayna Ccapac. After the Inca Tupac had rejoiced and celebrated the birthday festivals, although the four years were passed that his father had given him to complete the conquests, he heard that there was a great nation towards the South Sea, composed of Indians called Huancavelicas. So he determined to go down to conquer. At the head of the mountains above them he built the fortress of Huachalla, and then went down against the Huancavelicas. Tupac divided his army into three parts, and took one by the most rugged mountains, making war on the Huancavelica mountaineers. He penetrated so far into the mountains that for a long time nothing was known of him, whether he was dead or alive. He conquered the Huancavelicas although they were very warlike, fighting on land and at sea in balsas, from Tumbez to Huañapi, Huamo, Manta, Turuca and Quisin.

Marching and conquering on the coast of Manta, and the island of Puna, and Tumbez, there arrived at Tumbez some merchants who had come by sea from the west, navigating in balsas with sails. They gave information of the land whence they came, which consisted of some islands called Avachumbi and Ninachumbi, where there were many people and much gold. Tupac Inca was a man of lofty and ambitious ideas, and was not satisfied with the regions he had already conquered. So he determined to challenge a happy fortune, and see if it would favour him by sea. Yet he did not lightly believe the navigating merchants, for such men, being great talkers, ought not to be credited too readily. In order to obtain fuller information, and as it was not a business of which news could easily be got, he called a man, who accompanied him in his conquests, named Antarqui who, they all declare, was a great necromancer and could even fly through the air. Tupac Inca asked him whether what the merchant mariners said was true. Antarqui answered, after having thought the matter well out, that what they said was true, and that he would go there first. They say that he accomplished this by his arts, traversed the route, saw the islands, their people and riches, and, returning, gave certain information of all to Tupac Inca.

The Inca, having this certainty, determined to go there. He caused an immense number of balsas to be constructed, in which he embarked more than 20,000 chosen men; taking with him as captains Huaman Achachi, Cunti Yupanqui, Quihual Tupac (all Hanan-cuzcos), Yancan Mayta, Quisu Mayta, Cachimapaca Macus Yupanqui, Llimpita Usca Mayta (Hurin-cuzcos); his brother Tilca Yupanqui being general of the whole fleet. Apu Yupanqui was left in command of the army which remained on land.

Tupac Inca navigated and sailed on until he discovered the islands of Avachumbi and Ninachumbi, and returned, bringing back with him black people, gold, a chair of brass, and a skin and jaw bone of a horse. These trophies were preserved in the fortress of Cuzco until the Spaniards came. An Inca now living had charge of this skin and jaw bone of a horse. He gave this account, and the rest who were present corroborated it. His name is Urco Huaranca. I am particular about this because to those who know anything of the Indies it will appear a strange thing and difficult to believe. The duration of this expedition undertaken by Tupac Inca was nine months, others say a year, and, as he was so long absent, every one believed he was dead. But to deceive them and make them think that news of Tupac Inca had come, Apu Yupanqui, his general of the land army, made rejoicings. This was afterwards commented upon to his disadvantage, and it was said that he rejoiced because he was pleased that Tupac Inca Yupanqui did not appear. It cost him his life.

These are the islands which I discovered in the South Sea on the 30th of November, 1567, 200 and more leagues to the westward, being the great discovery of which I gave notice to the Licentiate Governor Castro. But Alvaro de Mendaña, General of the Fleet, did not wish to occupy them[104].

[Note 104: This story of the navigation of Tupac Inca to the islands of Ninachumbi and Avachumbi or Hahua chumpi is told by Balboa as well as by Sarmiento. They were no doubt two of the Galapagos Islands. Nina chumpi means fire island, and Hahua chumpi outer island. See my introduction to the Voyages of Sarmiento, p. xiii; and Las Islas de Galapagos by Marco Jimenes de la Espada.]

After Tupac Inca disembarked from the discovery of the islands, he proceeded to Tumipampa, to visit his wife and son and to hurry preparations for the return to Cuzco to see his father, who was reported to be ill. On the way back he sent troops along the coast to Truxillo, then called Chimu, where they found immense wealth of gold and silver worked into wands, and into beams of the house of Chimu Ccapac, with all which they joined the main army at Caxamarca. Thence Tupac Inca took the route to Cuzco, where he arrived after an absence of six years since he set out on this campaign.

Tupac Inca Yupanqui entered Cuzco with the greatest, the richest, and the most solemny triumph with which any Inca had ever reached the House of the Sun, bringing with him people of many different races, strange animals, innumerable quantities of riches. But behold the evil condition of Pachacuti Inca Yupanqui and his avarice, for though Tupac Inca was his son whose promotion he had procured, he felt such jealousy that his son should have gained such honour and fame in those conquests, that he publicly showed annoyance that it was not himself who triumphed, and that all was not due to him. So he determined to kill his sons Tilca Yupanqui and Auqui Yupanqui who had gone with Tupac Inca, their crime being that they had disobeyed his orders by delaying longer than the time he had fixed, and that they had taken his son to such a distance that he thought he would never return to Cuzco. They say that he killed them, though some say that he only killed Tilca Yupanqui. At this Tupac Inca Yupanqui felt much aggrieved, that his father should have slain one who had worked so well for him. The death was concealed by many feasts in honour of the victories of Tupac Inca, which were continued for a year.

XLVII.DEATH OF PACHACUTI INCA YUPANQUI.

Pachacuti Inca Yupanqui derived much comfort from his grandson, the son of Tupac Inca. He always had the child with him, and caused him to be brought up and cherished in his residence and dormitory. He would not let him out of his sight.

Being in the highest prosperity and sovereignty of his life, he fell ill of a grave infirmity, and, feeling that he was at the point of death, he sent for all his sons who were then in the city. In their presence he first divided all his jewels and contents of his wardrobe. Next he made them plough furrows in token that they were vassals of their brother, and that they had to eat by the sweat of their hands. He also gave them arms in token that they were to fight for their brother. He then dismissed them.

He next sent for the Incas orejones of Cuzco, his relations, and for Tupac Inca his son to whom he spoke, with a few words, in this manner:—"Son! you now see how many great nations I leave to you, and you know what labour they have cost me. Mind that you are the man to keep and augment them. No one must raise his two eyes against you and live, even if he be your own brother. I leave you these our relations that they may be your councillors. Care for them and they shall serve you. When I am dead, take care of my body, and put it in my houses at Patallacta. Have my golden image in the House of the Sun, and make my subjects, in all the provinces, offer up solemn sacrifice, after which keep the feast of purucaya, that I may go to rest with my father the Sun." Having finished his speech they say that he began to sing in a low and sad voice with words of his own language. They are in Castilian as follows:

"I was born as a flower of the field,
As a flower I was cherished in my youth,
I came to my full age, I grew old,
Now I am withered and die."

Having uttered these words, he laid his head upon a pillow and expired, giving his soul to the devil, having lived 125 years. For he succeeded, or rather he took the Incaship into his hands when he was 22, and he was sovereign 103 years.

He had four legitimate sons by his wife Mama Anahuarqui, and he had 100 sons and 50 daughters who were bastards. Being numerous they were called Hatun-ayllu, which means a "great lineage." By another name this lineage is called Inaca Panaca Ayllu. Those who sustain this lineage at the present time are Don Diego Cayo, Don Felipa Inguil, Don Juan Quispi Cusi, Don Francisco Chaco Rimachi, and Don Juan Illac. They live in Cuzco and are Hanan-cuzcos.

Pachacuti was a man of good stature, robust, fierce, haughty, insatiably bent on tyrannizing over all the world, [and cruel above measure. All the ordinances he made for the people were directed to tyranny and his own interests]. His conduct was infamous for he often took some widow as a wife and if she had a daughter that he liked, he also took the daughter for wife or concubine. If there was some gallant and handsome youth in the town who was esteemed for something, he presently made some of his servants make friends with him, get him into the country, and kill him the best way they could. He took all his sisters as concubines, saying they could not have a better husband than their brother.

This Inca died in the year 1191. He conquered more than 300 leagues, 40 more or less in person accompanied by his legitimate brothers, the captains Apu Mayta and Vicaquirao, the rest by Amaru Tupac Inca his eldest son, Ccapac Yupanqui his brother, and Tupac Inca his son and successor, with other captains, his brothers and sons.

This Inca arranged the parties and lineages of Cuzco in the order that they now are. The Licentiate Polo found the body of Pachacuti in Tococachi, where now is the parish of San Blas of the city of Cuzco, well preserved and guarded. He sent it to Lima by order of the Viceroy of this kingdom, the Marquis of Cañete. The guauqui or idol of this Inca was called Inti Illapa. It was of gold and very large, and was brought to Caxamarca in pieces. The Licentiate Polo found that this guauqui or idol had a house, estate, servants and women.

XLVIII. THE LIFE OF TUPAC INCA YUPANQUI[105], THE TENTH INCA.

[Note 105: All authorities agree that Tupac Inca Yupanqui was the successor of Pachacuti except Betanzos, Santillana and Garcilasso de la Vega. Betanzos has a Yamqui Yupanqui. Garcilasso gives the reign of another Inca named Inca Yupanqui between Pachacuti and Tupac Inca. He was ignorant of the fact that Pachacuti and Inca Yupanqui were the same person. Santillana follows Garcilasso but calls Pachacuti's other self Ccapac Yupanqui.]

When Pachacuti Inca Yupanqui died, two orejones were deputed to watch the body, and to allow no one to enter or go out to spread the news of his death, until orders had been given. The other Incas and orejones went with Tupac Inca to the House of the Sun and then ordered the twelve captains of the ayllus of the Inca's guard to come. They came with 2200 men of the guard, under their command, fully armed, and surrounded the Yupanqui with the fringe, and gave him the other insignia of sovereignty, as he had now inherited and succeeded his father. Taking him in the midst of themselves, and of the guards, they escorted him to the great square, where he was seated, in majesty, on a superb throne. All the people of the city were then ordered to come and make obeisance to the Inca on pain of death.

Those who had come with the Inca, went to their houses to fetch presents to show reverence and do homage to the new Inca. He remained with his guards only, until they returned with presents, doing homage and adoring. The rest of the people did the same, and sacrifices were offered. [It is to be noted that only those of Cuzco did this, and if any others were present who did so, they must have been forced or frightened by the armed men and the proclamation.]

This having been done, they approached the Inca and said, "O Sovereign Inca! O Father! now take rest." At these words Tupac Inca showed much sadness and covered his head with his mantle, which they call llacolla, a square cloak. He next went, with all his company, to the place where the body of his father was laid, and there he put on mourning. All things were then arranged for the obsequies, and Tupac Inca Yupanqui did everything that his father had ordered at the point of death, touching the treatment of his body and other things.

XLIX. TUPAC INCA YUPANQUI CONQUERS THE PROVINCE OF THE ANTIS.

Pachacuti Inca Yupanqui being dead, and Tupac Inca ruling alone, he caused all the Sinchis and principal men of the conquered provinces to be summoned. Those came who feared the fury of the Inca, and with them the Indians of the province of Anti-suyu, who are the dwellers in the forests to the eastward of Cuzco, who had been conquered in the time of Pachacuti his father. Tupac Inca ordered them all to do homage, adore, and offer sacrifices. The Antis were ordered to bring from their country several loads of lances of palm wood for the service of the House of the Sun. The Antis, who did not serve voluntarily, looked upon this demand as a mark of servitude. They fled from Cuzco, returned to their country, and raised the land of the Antis in the name of freedom.

Tupac Inca was indignant, and raised a powerful army which he divided into three parts. He led the first in person, entering the Anti-suyu by Ahua-tona. The second was entrusted to a captain named Uturuncu Achachi, who entered Anti-suyu by a town they call Amaru. The third, under a captain named Chalco Yupanqui, advanced by way of Pilcopata. All these routes were near each other, and the three divisions formed a junction three leagues within the forest, at a place called Opatari, whence they commenced operations against the settlements of the Antis. The inhabitants of this region were Antis, called Opataris, and were the first to be conquered. Chalco Yupanqui carried an image of the Sun.

The forests were very dense and full of evil places; so that they could not force their way through, nor did they know what direction to take in order to reach the settlements of the natives, which were well concealed in the thick vegetation. To find them the explorers climbed up the highest trees, and pointed out the places where they could see smoke rising. So they worked away at road making through the undergrowth until they lost that sign of inhabitants and found another. In this way the Inca made a road where it seemed impossible to make one.

The Sinchi of the greater part of these provinces of the Antis was Condin Savana, of whom they say that he was a great wizard and enchanter, and they had the belief, and even now they affirm that he could turn himself into different shapes.

Tupac Inca and his captains penetrated into this region of the Antis, which consists of the most terrible and fearful forests, with many rivers, where they endured immense toil, and the people who came from Peru suffered from the change of climate, for Peru is cold and dry, while the forests of Anti-suyu are warm and humid. The soldiers of Tupac Inca became sick, and many died. Tupac Inca himself, with a third of his men who came with him to conquer, were lost in the forests, and wandered for a long time, without knowing whether to go in one direction or another until he fell in with Uturuncu Achachi who put him on the route.

On this occasion Tupac Inca and his captains conquered four great tribes. The first was that of the Indians called Opataris. The next was the Mano-suyu. The third tribe was called Mañaris or Yanasimis, which means those of the black mouth: and the province of Rio, and the province of the Chunchos. They went over much ground in descending the river Tono, and penetrated as far as the Chiponauas. The Inca sent another great captain, named Apu Ccuri-machi, by the route which they now call of Camata. This route was in the direction of the rising of the sun, and he advanced until he came to the river of which reports have but now been received, called Paytiti, where he set up the frontier pillars of Inca Tupac. During the campaign against these nations, Tupac Inca took prisoners the following Sinchis: Vinchincayua, Cantahuancuru, Nutan-huari[106].

[Note 106: This expedition of Tupac Inca Yupanqui into the montaña of Paucartambo, and down the River Tono is important. Garcilasso de la Vega describes it in chapters xiii., xiv., xv. and xvi. of Book vii. He says that five rivers unite to form the great Amaru-mayu or Serpent River, which he was inclined to think was a tributary of the Rio de la Plata. He describes fierce battles with the Chunchos, who were reduced to obedience. After descending the River Tono, Garcilasso says that the Incas eventually reached the country of the Musus (Moxos) and opened friendly relations with them. Many Incas settled in the country of the Musus. Garcilasso then gives some account of Spanish expeditions into the montaña, led by Diego Aleman, Gomez de Tordoya, and Juan Alvarez Maldonado.

The account in the text agrees, in the main, with that of Garcilasso de la Vega. Sarmiento gives the names of four Indian tribes who were encountered, besides the Chunchos.]

During the campaign an Indian of the Collas, named Coaquiri, fled from his company, reached the Collao, and spread the report that Tupac Inca was dead. He said that there was no longer an Inca, that they should all rise and that he would be their leader. Presently he took the name of Pachacuti, the Collas rose, and chose him as their captain. This news reached Tupac Inca in Anti-suyu where he was in the career of conquest. He resolved to march against the Collas and punish them. He left the forests, leaving Uturuncu Achachi to complete the conquest, with orders to return into Peru when that service was completed, but not to enter Cuzco triumphing until the Inca should come.

L.TUPAC INCA YUPANQUI GOES TO SUBDUE AND PACIFY THE COLLAS.

As the Collas were one of those nations which most desired their freedom, they entered upon attempts to obtain it whenever a chance offered, as has already been explained. Tupac Inca Yupanqui resolved to crush them once for all. Having returned from the Antis, he increased his army and nominated as captains Larico, the son of his cousin Ccapac Yupanqui, his brother Chachi, Cunti Yupanqui, and Quihual Tupac. With this army he advanced to the Collao. The Collas had constructed four strong places at Llallaua, Asillo, Arapa, and Pucara. The Inca captured the chiefs and the leader of all, who was Chuca-chucay Pachacuti Coaquiri, he who, as we have said, fled from Anti-suyu. Afterwards these were the drummers[107] of Inca Tupac. Finally, owing to the great diligence of Inca Tupac, although the war occupied some years, the Incas conquered and subdued all [perpetrating great cruelties on them].

Following up his victories, in pursuit of the vanquished, he got so far from Cuzco that he found himself in Charcas. So he determined to advance further, subduing every nation of which he received notice. He eventually prosecuted his conquests so far that he entered Chile, where he defeated the great Sinchi Michimalongo, and Tangalongo, Sinchi of the Chilians as far as the river Maule. He came to Coquimbo in Chile and to the banks of the Maule, where he set up his frontier columns, or as others say a wall, to show the end of his conquests. From this campaign he returned with great riches in gold, having discovered many mines of gold and silver. He then returned to Cuzco.

These spoils were joined with those of Uturuncu Achachi, who had returned from the forests of the Antis after a campaign of three years. He was at Paucar-tampu, awaiting the return of his brother, who entered Cuzco with a very great triumph. They made great feasts to commemorate the conquests, presenting gifts and granting many favours to the soldiers who had served with the Inca in these campaigns. As the provinces of the Chumpi-vilicas saw the power and greatness of Tupac Inca Yupanqui they came to submit with the rest of Cunti-suyu.

[Note 107: i.e. their skins were made into drums.]

Besides this the Inca went to Chachapoyas, and crushed those who had been suspected, visiting many provinces on the road.

On his return to Cuzco he made certain ordinances, as well for peace as for war time. He increased the mitimaes which his father had instituted, as has been explained in the account of his life, giving more privileges and liberty. Besides, he caused a general visitation to be made of all the land from Quito to Chile, registering the whole population for more than a thousand leagues; and imposed a tribute [so heavy that no one could be owner of a mazorca of maize, which is their bread for food, nor of a pair of usutas, which are their shoes, nor marry, nor do a single thing without special licence from Tupac Inca. Such was the tyranny and oppression to which he subjected them]. He placed over the tucuricos a class of officers called Michu[108] to collect the taxes and tributes.

[Note 108: Michu should be Michec a shepherd, also a governor. Michisca the governed.]

Tupac Inca saw that in the districts and provinces the Sinchis claimed to inherit by descent. He resolved to abolish this rule, and to put them all under his feet, both great and small. He, therefore, deposed the existing Sinchis, and introduced a class of ruler at his own will, who were selected in the following way. He appointed a ruler who should have charge of 10,000 men, and called him huanu, which means that number. He appointed another ruler over 1000, and called him huaranca, which is 1000. The next had charge of 500, called pichca-pachaca, or 500. To another called pachac he gave charge of 100, and to another he gave charge of 10 men, called chunca curaca. All these had also the title of Curaca, which means "principal" or "superior," over the number of men of whom they had charge. These appointments depended solely on the will of the Inca, who appointed and dismissed them as he pleased, without considering inheritance, or succession. From that time forward they were called Curacas, which is the proper name of the chiefs of this land, and not Caciques, which is the term used by the vulgar among the Spaniards. That name of Cacique belongs to the islands of Santo Domingo and Cuba. From this place we will drop the name of Sinchi and only use that of Curaca.

LI. TUPAC INCA MAKES THE YANACONAS.

Among the brothers of the Inca there was one named Tupac Ccapac, a principal man, to whom Tupac Inca had given many servants to work on his farms, and serve on his estates. It is to be understood that Tupac Inca made his brother visitor-general of the whole empire that had been conquered up to that time. Tupac Ccapac, in making the visitation, came to the place where his brother had given him those servants. Under colour of this grant, he took those and also many more, saying that all were his yana-cunas[109], which is the name they give to their servants. He persuaded them to rebel against his brother, saying that if they would help him he would show them great favours. He then marched to Cuzco, very rich and powerful, where he gave indications of his intentions.

[Note 109: Garcilasso de la Vega says that the meaning of Yanacona is "a man who is under the obligation to perform the duties of a servant." Balboa, p. 129, tells the same story of the origin of the Yanaconas as in the text. The amnesty was granted on the banks of the river Yana-yacu, and here they were called Yana-yacu-cuna, corrupted into Yana-cona. The Spaniards adopted the word for all Indians in domestic service, as distinguished from mitayos or forced labourers.]

He intended his schemes to be kept secret, but Tupac Inca was informed of them and came to Cuzco. He had been away at the ceremony of arming one of his sons named Ayar Manco. Having convinced himself that his information was correct, he killed Tupac Ccapac with all his councillors and supporters. Finding that many tribes had been left out of the visitation by him, for this attempt, Tupac Inca went in person from Cuzco, to investigate the matter and finish the visitation.

While doing this the Inca came to a place called Yana-yacu, which means "black water" because a stream of a very dark colour flows down that valley, and for that reason they call the river and valley Yana-yacu. Up to this point he had been inflicting very cruel punishment without pardoning any one who was found guilty either in word or deed. In this valley of Yana-yacu his sister and wife, Mama Ocllo, asked him not to continue such cruelties, which were more butchery and inhumanity than punishment, and not to kill any more but to pardon them, asking for them as her servants. In consequence of this intercession, the Inca ceased the slaughter, and said that he would grant a general pardon. As the pardon was proclaimed in Yana-yacu, he ordered that all the pardoned should be called Yana-yacus. They were known as not being allowed to enter in the number of servants of the House of the Sun, nor those of the visitation. So they remained under the Curacas. This affair being finished, the visitation made by Tupac Ccapac was considered to be of no effect. So the Inca returned to Cuzco with the intention of ordering another visitation to be made afresh.

LII.TUPAC INCA YUPANQUI ORDERS A SECOND VISITATION OF THE LAND, AND DOES OTHER THINGS.

As the visitation entrusted to Tupac Ccapac was not to his liking, the Inca revoked it, and nominated another brother named Apu Achachi to be visitor-general. The Inca ordered him not to include the Yana-yacus in the visitation, because they were unworthy to enter into the number of the rest, owing to what they had done, Apu Achachi set out and made his general visitation, reducing many of the Indians to live in villages and houses who had previously lived in caves and hills and on the banks of rivers, each one by himself. He sent those in strong fastnesses into plains, that they might have no site for a fortress, on the strength of which they might rebel. He reduced them into provinces, giving them their Curacas in the order already described. He did not make the son of the deceased a Curaca, but the man who had most ability and aptitude for the service. If the appointment did not please the Inca he, without more ado, dismissed him and appointed another, so that no Curaca, high or low, felt secure in his appointment. To these Curacas were given servants, women and estates, submitting an account of them, for, though they were Curacas, they could not take a thing of their own authority, without express leave from the Inca.

In each province all those of the province made a great sowing of every kind of edible vegetable for the Inca, his overseers coming to the harvest. Above all there was a Tucurico Apu, who was the governor-lieutenant of the Inca in that province. It is true that the first Inca who obliged the Indians of this land to pay tribute of everything, and in quantity, was Inca Yupanqui. But Tupac Inca imposed rules and fixed the tribute they must pay, and divided it according to what each province was to contribute as well for the general tax as those for Huacas, and Houses of the Sun. [In this way the people were so loaded with tributes and taxes, that they had to work perpetually night and day to pay them, and even then they could not comply, and had no time for sufficient labour to suffice for their own maintenance.]

Tupac Inca divided the estates throughout the whole empire, according to the measure which they call tupu.

He divided the months of the year, with reference to labour in the fields, as follows. Three months in the year were allotted to the Indians for the work of their own fields, and the rest must be given up to the work of the Sun, of huacas, and of the Inca. In the three months that were given to themselves, one was for ploughing and sowing, one for reaping, and another in the summer for festivals, and for make and mend clothes days. The rest of their time was demanded for the service of the Sun and the Incas.

This Inca ordered that there should be merchants who might profit by their industry in this manner. When any merchant brought gold, silver, precious stones, or other valuable things for sale, they were to be asked where they got them, and in this way they gave information respecting the mines and places whence the valuables had been taken. Thus a very great many mines of gold and silver, and of very fine colours, were discovered.

This Inca had two Governors-General in the whole empire, called Suyuyoc Apu[110]; one resided at Xauxa and the other at Tiahuanacu in

Colla-suyu.

[Note 110: Suyu a great division of the empire, or a province. Yoc a terminal particle denoting possession or office.]

Tupac Inca ordered the seclusion of certain women in the manner of our professed nuns, maidens of 12 years and upwards, who were called acllas[111]. From thence they were taken to be given in marriage to the Tucurico Apu, or by order of the Inca who, when any captain returned with victory, distributed the acllas to captains, soldiers and other servants who had pleased him, as gracious gifts which were highly valued. As they took out some, they were replaced by others, for there must always be the number first ordained by the Inca. If any man takes one out, or is caught inside with one they are both hanged, tied together.

[Note 111: Aclla means chosen, selected.]

This Inca made many ordinances, in his tyrannical mode of government, which will be given in a special volume.

LIII.TUPAC INCA MAKES THE FORTRESS OF CUZCO.

After Tupac Inca Yupanqui had visited all the empire and had come to Cuzco where he was served and adored, being for the time idle, he remembered that his father Pachacuti had called the city of Cuzco the lion city. He said that the tail was where the two rivers unite which flow through it[112], that the body was the great square and the houses round it, and that the head was wanting. It would be for some son of his to put it on. The Inca discussed this question with the orejones, who said that the best head would be to make a fortress on a high plateau to the north of the city.

[Note 112: This district of Cuzco has always been called Pumap chupan or tail of the puma.]

This being settled, the Inca sent to all the provinces, to order the tucuricos to supply a large number of people for the work of the fortress. Having come, the workmen were divided into parties, each one having its duties and officers. Thus some brought stones, others worked them, others placed them. The diligence was such that in a few years, the great fortress of Cuzco was built, sumptuous, exceedingly strong, of rough stone, a thing most admirable to look upon. The buildings within it were of small worked stone, so beautiful that, if it had not been seen, it would not be believed how strong and beautiful it was. What makes it still more worthy of admiration is that they did not possess tools to work the stone, but could only work with other stones. This fortress was intact until the time of the differences between Pizarro and Almagro, after which they began to dismantle it, to build with its stones the houses of Spaniards in Cuzco, which are at the foot of the fortress. Great regret is felt by those who see the ruins. When it was finished, the Inca made many store houses round Cuzco for provisions and clothing, against times of necessity and of war; which was a measure of great importance[113].

[Note 113: This fortress of Cuzco, on the Sacsahuaman Hill, was well described by Cieza de Leon and in greater detail by Garcilasso de la Vega, ii. pp. 305—318. Both ascribe it to Inca Yupanqui or his son Tupac Inca, as does Sarmiento. The extensive edifices, built of masonry of his period, were no doubt the work of Tupac Inca who thus got credit for the whole. These later edifices were pulled down by the Spaniards, for material for building their houses in the city. But the wonderful cyclopean work that remains is certainly of much more ancient date, and must be assigned, like Tiahuanacu, to the far distant age of the monolithic empire.]

LIV.DEATH OF TUPAC INCA YUPANQUI.

Having visited and divided the lands, and built the fortress of Cuzco, besides edifices and houses without number, Tupac Inca Yupanqui went to Chinchero[114], a town near Cuzco, where he had very rich things for his recreation; and there he ordered extensive gardens to be constructed to supply his household. When the work was completed he fell ill of a grave infirmity, and did not wish to be visited by anyone. But as he became worse and felt the approach of death, he sent for the orejones of Cuzco, his relations, and when they had assembled in his presence he said: "My relations and friends! I would have you to know that the Sun my Father desires to take me to himself, and I wish to go and rest with him. I have called you to let you know who it is that I desire to succeed me as lord and sovereign, and who is to rule and govern you." They answered that they grieved much at his illness, that as the Sun his father had so willed it so must it be, that his will must be done, and they besought the Inca to nominate him who was to be sovereign in his place. Tupac Inca then replied: "I nominate for my successor my son Titu Cusi Hualpa, son of my sister and wife, Mama Ocllo." For this they offered many thanks, and afterwards the Inca sank down on his pillow and died, having lived 85 years.

[Note 114: Chinchero is a village near Cuzco, on the heights overlooking the lovely valley of Yucay, with magnificent mountains in the background. The remains of the Inca palace are still standing, not unlike those on the Colcampata at Cuzco.]

Tupac Inca succeeded his father at the age of 18 years. He had two legitimate sons, 60 bastards, and 30 daughters. Some say that at the time of his death, or a short time before, he had nominated one of his illegitimate sons to succeed him named Ccapac Huari, son of a concubine whose name was Chuqui Ocllo.

He left a lineage or ayllu called Ccapac Ayllu, whose heads, who sustain it and are now living, are Don Andres Tupac Yupanqui, Don Cristobal Pisac Tupac, Don Garcia Vilcas, Don Felipe Tupac Yupanqui, Don Garcia Azache, and Don Garcia Pilco. They are Hanan-cuzcos.

The deceased Inca was frank, merciful in peace, cruel in war and punishments, a friend to the poor, a great man of indefatigable industry and a notable builder. [He was the greatest tyrant of all the Incas.] He died in the year 1528. Chalco Chima burnt his body in 1533, when he captured Huascar, as will be related in its place. The ashes, with his idol or guauqui called Cusi-churi, were found in Calis-puquiu where the Indians had concealed it, and offered to it many sacrifices.

LV. THE LIFE OF HUAYNA CCAPAC, ELEVENTH INCA[115].

[Note 115: All authorities agree that Huayna Ccapac was the son and successor of Tupac Inca.]

As soon as Tupac Inca was dead, the orejones, who were with him at the time of his death, proceeded to Cuzco for the customary ceremonies. These were to raise the Inca his successor before the death of his father had become known to him, and to follow the same order as in the case of the death of Pachacuti Inca Yupanqui. As the wives and sons of Tupac Inca also went to Cuzco, the matter could not be kept secret. A woman who had been a concubine of the late Inca, named Ccuri Ocllo, a kins-woman of Ccapac Huari, as soon as she arrived at Cuzco, spoke to her relations and to Ccapac Huari in these words. "Sirs and relations! Know that Tupac Inca is dead and that, when in health, he had named Ccapac Huari for his successor, but at the end, being on the point of death, he said that Titu Cusi Hualpa, son of Mama Ocllo, should succeed him. You ought not to consent to this. Rather call together all your relations and friends, and raise Ccapac Huari, your elder brother, son of Chuqui Ocllo, to be Inca." This seemed well to all the relations of Ccapac Huari, and they sent to assemble all the other relations on his behalf.

While this was proceeding, the orejones of Cuzco, knowing nothing of it, were arranging how to give the fringe to Titu Cusi Hualpa. The plot of the party of Ccapac Huari became known to the late Inca's brother, Huaman Achachi. He assembled some friends, made them arm themselves, and they went to where Titu Cusi Hualpa was retired and concealed. They then proceeded to where the friends of Ccapac Huari had assembled, and killed many of them, including Ccapac Huari himself. Others say that they did not kill Ccapac Huari at that time, but only took him. His mother Chuqui Ocllo was taken and, being a rebel as well as a witch who had killed her lord Tupac Inca, she was put to death. Ccapac Huari was banished to Chinchero, where he was given a maintenance, but he was never allowed to enter Cuzco again until his death. They also killed the woman Ccuri Ocllo, who had advised the raising of Ccapac Huari to the Incaship.

LVI.THEY GIVE THE FRINGE OF INCA TO HUAYNA CCAPAC, THE ELEVENTH INCA.

The city of Cuzco being pacified, Huaman Achachi went to Quispicancha, three leagues from Cuzco, where Titu Cusi Hualpa was concealed, and brought his nephew to Cuzco, to the House of the Sun. After the sacrifices and accustomed ceremonies, the image of the Sun delivered the fringe to Titu Cusi Hualpa.

This being done, and the new Inca having been invested with all the insignia of Ccapac, and placed in a rich litter, they bore him to the huaca Huanacauri, where he offered a sacrifice. The orejones returned to Cuzco by the route taken by Manco Ccapac.

Arrived at the first square, called Rimac-pampa, the accession was announced to the people, and they were ordered to come and do homage to the new Inca. When they all assembled, and saw how young he was, never having seen him before, they all raised their voices and called him Huayna Ccapac which means "the boy chief" or "the boy sovereign." For this reason he was called Huayna Ccapac from that time, and the name Titu Cusi Hualpa was no longer used. They celebrated festivals, armed him as a knight, adored, and presented many gifts—as was customary.

LVII.THE FIRST ACTS OF HUAYNA CCAPAC AFTER HE BECAME INCA.

As Huayna Ccapac was very young when he succeeded, they appointed a tutor and coadjutor for him named Hualpaya, a son of Ccapac Yupanqui, brother of Inca Yupanqui. This prince made a plot to raise himself to the Incaship, but it became known to Huaman Achachi, then Governor of Chinchay-suyu. At the time he was in Cuzco, and he and his people killed Hualpaya and others who were culpable.

Huaman Achachi assumed the government, but always had as a councillor his own brother Auqui Tupac Inca. In course of time Huayna Ccapac went to the House of the Sun, held a visitation, took account of the officials, and provided what was necessary for the service, and for that of the Mama-cunas. He took the chief custodianship of the Sun from him who then held it, and assumed the office himself with the title of "Shepherd of the Sun." He next visited the other huacas and oracles, and their estates. He also inspected the buildings of the city of Cuzco and the houses of the orejones.

Huayna Ccapac ordered the body of his father Tupac Inca to be embalmed. After the sacrifices, the mourning, and other ceremonies, he placed the body in the late Inca's residence which was prepared for it, and gave his servants all that was necessary for their maintenance and services. The same Huayna Ccapac mourned for his father and for his mother who died nearly at the same time.

LVIII.HUAYNA CCAPAC CONQUERS CHACHAPOYAS.

After Huayna Ccapac had given orders respecting the things mentioned in the last chapter, it was reported to him that there were certain tribes near the territory of the Chachapoyas which might be conquered, and that on the way he might subdue the Chachapoyas who had rebelled. He gave orders to his orejones and assembled a large army. He set out from Cuzco, having first offered sacrifices and observed the calpa[116]. On the route he took, he reformed many things. Arriving at the land of the Chachapoyas, they, with other neighbouring tribes, put themselves in a posture of defence. They were eventually vanquished and treated with great severity. The Inca then returned to Cuzco and triumphed at the victory gained over the Chachapoyas and other nations.

[Note 116: Calpa means force, power. Calpay work. Calparicu "one who gives strength," used for a wizard. The Calpa was a ceremony connected with divination.]

While he was absent on this campaign, he left as Governor of Cuzco one of his illegitimate brothers named Sinchi Rocca, an eminent architect. He built all the edifices at Yucay, and the houses of the Inca at Casana in the city of Cuzco. He afterwards built other edifices round Cuzco for Huayna Ccapac, on sites which appeared most convenient.

LIX.HUAYNA CCAPAC MAKES A VISITATION OF THE WHOLE EMPIRE FROM QUITO TO CHILE.

Huayna Ccapac having rested in Cuzco for a long time and, wishing to undertake something, considered that it was a long time since he had visited the empire. He determined that there should be a visitation, and named his uncle Huaman Achachi to conduct it in Chinchay-suyu as far as Quito, he himself undertaking the region of Colla-suyu.

Each one set out, Huayna Ccapac, in person, taking the route to the Collao, where he examined into the government of his tucuricos, placing and dismissing governors and Curacas, opening lands and making bridges and irrigating channels. Constructing these works he arrived at Charcas and went thence to Chile, which his father had conquered, where he dismissed the governor, and appointed two native Curacas named Michimalongo and Antalongo, who had been vanquished by his father. Having renewed the garrison, he came to Coquimbo and Copiapo, also visiting Atacama and Arequipa. He next went to Anti-suyu and Alayda, by way of Collao and Charcas. He entered the valley of Cochabamba, and there made provinces of mitimaes in all parts, because the natives were few, and there was space for all, the land being fertile. Thence he went to Pocona to give orders on that frontier against the Chirihuanas, and to repair a fortress which had been built by his father.

While engaged on these measures, he received news that the provinces of Quito, Cayambis, Carangues, Pastos, and Huancavilcas had rebelled. He, therefore, hurried his return and came to Tiahuanacu, where he prepared for war against the Quitos and Cayambis, and gave orders how the Urus[117] were to live, granting them localities in which each tribe of them was to fish in the lake. He visited the Temple of the Sun and the huaca of Ticci Viracocha on the island of Titicaca, and sent orders that all those provinces should send troops to go to that war which he had proclaimed.

[Note 117: The Urus are a tribe of fishermen, with a peculiar language, living among the reed beds in the S.W. part of Lake Titicaca.]

LX.HUAYNA CCAPAC MAKES WAR ON THE QUITOS, PASTOS,

CARANGUES, CAYAMBIS, HUANCAVILCAS.

Knowing that the Pastos, Quitos, Carangues, Cayambis and Huancavilcas had rebelled, killed the tucuricos, and strengthened their positions with strong forces, Huayna Ccapac, with great rapidity, collected a great army from all the districts of the four suyus. He nominated Michi of the Hurin-cuzcos, and Auqui Tupac of the Hanan-cuzcos as captains, and left his uncle Huaman Achachi as governor of Cuzco. Others say that he left Apu Hilaquito and Auqui Tupac Inca in Cuzco, with his son who was to succeed named Tupac Cusi Hualpa Inti Illapa, and with him another of his sons named Titu Atanchi, who remained to perform the fasts before knighthood. It is to be noted that Huayna Ccapac was married, in conformity with custom and with the prescribed ceremonies to Cusi Rimay Coya, by whom he had no male child. He, therefore, took his sister Araua Ocllo to wife, by whom he had a son Tupac Cusi Hualpa, vulgarly called Huascar. Preparing for the campaign he ordered that Atahualpa and Ninan Cuyoche, his illegitimate sons, now grown men, should go with him. His other sons, also illegitimate, named Manco Inca and Paulu Tupac, were to remain with Huascar.

These arrangements having been made, the Inca set out for Quito. On the way he came to Tumipampa where he had himself been born. Here he erected great edifices where he placed, with great solemnity, the caul in which he was born. Marching onwards and reaching the boundary of the region where the Quitos were in arms, he marshalled his squadrons, and presently resolved to conquer the Pastos. For this service he selected two captains of the Collao, one named Mollo Cavana, the other Mollo Pucara, and two others of Cunti-suyu named Apu Cautar Cañana and Cunti Mollo, under whose command he placed many men of their nations, and 2000 orejones as guards, under Auqui Tupac Inca, brother of Huayna Ccapac and Acollo Tupac of the lineage of Viracocha. They marched to the country of the Pastos who fell back on their chief place, leaving their old people, women and children, with a few men, that the enemy might think there was no one else. The Incas easily conquered these and, thinking that was all, they gave themselves up to idleness and pleasure. One night, when they were engaged in a great rejoicing, eating and drinking freely, without sentries, the Pastos attacked them, and there was a great slaughter, especially among the Collas. Those who escaped, fled until they came to the main army of the Incas which was following them. They say that Atahualpa and Ninan Cuyoche brought up assistance, and that, with the confidence thus gained, Huayna Ccapac ordered the war to be waged most cruelly. So they entered the country of the Pastos a second time, burning and destroying the inhabited places and killing all the people great and small, men and women, young and old. That province having been subdued, a governor was appointed to it.

Huayna Ccapac then returned to Tumipampa, where he rested some days, before moving his camp for the conquest of the Carangues, a very warlike nation. In this campaign he subdued the Macas to the confines of the Cañaris, those of Quisna, of Ancamarca, the province of Puruvay, the Indians of Nolitria, and other neighbouring nations.

Thence he went down to Tumbez, a seaport, and then came to the fortresses of Carangui and Cochisque. In commencing to subdue those of Cochisque he met with a stubborn resistance by valiant men, and many were killed on both sides. At length the place was taken, and the men who escaped were received in the fortress of Carangui. The Incas decided that the country surrounding this fortress should first be subdued. They desolated the country as far as Ancasmayu and Otabalo, those who escaped from the fury of the Incas taking refuge in the fortress. Huayna Ccapac attacked it with his whole force, but was repulsed by the garrison with much slaughter, and the orejones were forced to fly, defeated by the Cayambis, the Inca himself being thrown down. He would have been killed if a thousand of his guard had not come up with their captains Cusi Tupac Yupanqui and Huayna Achachi, to rescue and raise him. The sight of this animated the orejones. All turned to defend their Inca, and pressed on with such vigour that the Cayambis were driven back into their fortress. The Inca army, in one encounter and the other, suffered heavy loss.

Huayna Ccapac, on this account, returned to Tumipampa, where he recruited his army, preparing to resume the attack on the Cayambis. At this time some orejones deserted the Inca, leaving him to go back to Cuzco. Huayna Ccapac satisfied the rest by gifts of clothes, provisions, and other things, and he formed an efficient army.

It was reported that the Cayambis had sallied from their fortress and had defeated a detachment of the Inca army, killing many, and the rest escaping by flight. This caused great sorrow to the Inca, who sent his brother Auqui Toma, with an army composed of all nations, against the Cayambis of the fortress. Auqui Toma went, attacked the fortress, captured four lines of defence and the outer wall, which was composed of five. But at the entrance the Cayambis killed Auqui Toma, captain of the Cuzcos, who had fought most valorously. This attack and defence was so obstinate and long continued that an immense number of men fell, and the survivors had nowhere to fight except upon heaps of dead men. The desire of both sides to conquer or die was so strong that they gave up their lances and arrows and took to their fists. At last, when they saw that their captain was killed, the Incas began to retreat towards a river, into which they went without any care for saving their lives. The river was in flood and a great number of men were drowned. This was a heavy loss for the cause of Huayna Ccapac. Those who escaped from drowning and from the hands of the enemy, sent the news to the Inca from the other side of the river. Huayna Ccapac received the news of this reverse with heavier grief than ever, for he dearly loved his brother Auqui Toma, who had been killed with so many men who were the pick of the army.

Huayna Ccapac was a brave man, and was not dismayed. On the contrary it raised his spirit and he resolved to be avenged. He again got ready his forces and marched in person against the fortress of the Cayambis. He formed the army in three divisions. He sent Michi with a third of the army to pass on one side of the fortress without being seen. This detachment consisted of Cuzco orejones, and men of Chinchay-suyu. They were to advance five marches beyond the fortress and, at a fixed time, return towards it, desolating and destroying. The Inca, with the rest of his army marched direct to the attack of the fortress, and began to fight with great fury. This continued some days, during which the Inca lost some men. While the battle was proceeding, Michi and those of Chinchay-suyu turned, desolating and destroying everything in the land of the Cayambis. They were so furious that they did not leave anything standing, making the very earth to tremble. When Huayna Ccapac knew that his detachment was near the fortress, he feigned a flight. The Cayambis, not aware of what was happening in their rear, came out of the fortress in pursuit of the Inca. When the Cayambis were at some distance from their stronghold, the Chinchay-suyus, commanded by Michi, came in sight. These met with no resistance in the fortress as the Cayambis were outside, following Huayna Ccapac. They easily entered it and set it on fire in several parts, killing or capturing all who were inside.

The Cayambis were, by this time, fighting with the army of Huayna Ccapac. When they saw their fortress on fire they lost hope and fled from the battle field towards a lake which was near, thinking that they could save themselves by hiding among the beds of reeds. But Huayna Ccapac followed them with great rapidity. In order that none might escape he gave instructions that the lake should be surrounded. In that lake, and the swamps on its borders, the troops of Huayna Ccapac, he fighting most furiously in person, made such havock and slaughter, that the lake was coloured with the blood of the dead Cayambis. From that time forward the lake has been called Yahuar-cocha, which means the "lake of blood," from the quantity that was there shed.

It is to be noted that in the middle of this lake there was an islet with two willow trees, up which some Cayambis climbed, and among them their two chiefs named Pinto and Canto, most valiant Indians. The troops of Huayna Ccapac pelted them with stones and captured Canto, but Pinto escaped with a thousand brave Cañaris.

The Cayambis being conquered, the Cuzcos began to select those who would look best in the triumphal entry into Cuzco. But they, thinking that they were being selected to be killed, preferred rather to die like men than to be tied up like women. So they turned and began to fight. Huayna Ccapac saw this and ordered them all to be killed.

The Inca placed a garrison in the fortress, and sent a captain with a detachment in pursuit of Pinto who, in his flight, was doing much mischief. They followed until Pinto went into forests, with other fugitives, escaping for a time. After Huayna Ccapac had rested for some days at Tumipampa, he got information where Pinto was in the forests, and surrounded them, closing up all entrances and exits. Hunger then obliged him, and those who were with him, to surrender. This Pinto was very brave and he had such hatred against Huayna Ccapac that even, after his capture, when the Inca had presented him with gifts and treated him kindly, he never could see his face. So he died out of his mind, and Huayna Ccapac ordered a drum to be made of his skin. The drum was sent to Cuzco, and so this war came to an end. It was at Cuzco in the taqui or dance in honour of the Sun.

LXI. THE CHIRIHUANAS COME TO MAKE WAR IN PERU AGAINST THOSE CONQUERED BY THE INCAS.

While Huayna Ccapac was occupied with this war of the Cayambis, the Chirihuanas, who form a nation of the forests, naked and eaters of human flesh, for which they have a public slaughter house, uniting, and, coming forth from their dense forests, entered the territory of Charcas, which had been conquered by the Incas of Peru. They attacked the fortress of Cuzco-tuyo, where the Inca had a large frontier garrison to defend the country against them. Their assault being sudden they entered the fortress, massacred the garrison, and committed great havock, robberies and murders among the surrounding inhabitants.

The news reached Huayna Ccapac at Quito, and he received it with much heaviness. He sent a captain, named Yasca, to Cuzco to collect troops, and with them to march against the Chirihuanas. This captain set out for Cuzco, taking with him the huaca "Cataquilla[118]" of Caxamarca and Huamachuco, and "Curichaculla" of the Chachapoyas; and the huacas "Tomayrica and Chinchay-cocha," with many people, the attendants of the huacas. He arrived at Cuzco where he was very well received by the Governors, Apu Hilaquito and Auqui Tupac Inca. Having collected his troops he left Cuzco for Charcas. On the road he enlisted many men of the Collao. With these he came up with the Chirihuanas and made cruel war upon them. He captured some to send to Huayna Ccapac at Quito, that the Inca might see what these strange men were like. The captain Yasca rebuilt the fortress and, placing in it the necessary garrison, he returned to Cuzco, dismissed his men, and each one returned to his own land.

[Note 118: It was the policy of the Incas that the idols and huacas of conquered nations should be sent to Cuzco and deposited there. Catiquilla was an idol of the Caxamarca and Huamachuco people. Arriaga calls it Apu-cati-quilla. Apu the great or chief, catic follower, quilla the moon. Apu-cati-quilla appears to have been a moon god. The other huacas are local deities, all sent to Cuzco. Catiquilla had been kept as an oracle in the village of Tauca in Conchucos (Calancha, p.

471). Cati-quilla would mean "following moon." (See also Extirpation de la idolatria del Peru, Joseph de Arriaga. Lima, 1627.)]

LXII.WHAT HUAYNA CCAPAC DID AFTER THE SAID WARS.

As soon as Huayna Ccapac had despatched the captain against the Chirihuanas, he set out from Tumipampa to organize the nations he had conquered, including Quito, Pasto, and Huancavilcas. He came to the river called Ancas-mayu, between Pasto and Quito, where he set up his boundary pillars at the limit of the country he had conquered. As a token of grandeur and as a memorial he placed certain golden staves in the pillars. He then followed the course of the river in search of the sea, seeking for people to conquer, for he had information that in that direction the country was well peopled.

On this road the army of the Inca was in great peril, suffering from scarcity of water, for the troops had to cross extensive tracts of sand. One day, at dawn, the Inca army found itself surrounded by an immense crowd of people, not knowing who they were. In fear of the unknown enemy, the troops began to retreat towards the Inca. Just as they were preparing for flight a boy came to Huayna Ccapac, and said: "My Lord! fear not, those are the people for whom we are in search. Let us attack them." This appeared to the Inca to be good advice and he ordered an impetuous attack to be made, promising that whatever any man took should be his. The orejones delivered such an assault on those who surrounded them that, in a short time, the circle was broken. The enemy was routed, and the fugitives made for their habitations, which were on the sea coast towards Coaques, where the Incas captured an immense quantity of rich spoils, emeralds, turquoises, and great store of very fine mollo, a substance formed in sea shells, more valued amongst them than gold or silver.

Here the Inca received a message from the Sinchi or Curaca of the island of Puna with a rich present, inviting him to come to his island to receive his service. Huayna Ccapac did so. Thence he went to Huancavilca, where he joined the reserves who had been left there. News came to him that a great pestilence was raging at Cuzco of which the governors Apu Hilaquito his uncle, and Auqui Tupac Inca his brother had died, also his sister Mama Cuca, and many other relations. To establish order among the conquered nations, the Inca went to Quito, intending to proceed from thence to Cuzco to rest.

On reaching Quito the Inca was taken ill with a fever, though others say it was small-pox or measles. He felt the disease to be mortal and sent for the orejones his relations, who asked him to name his successor. His reply was that his son Ninan Cuyoche was to succeed, if the augury of the calpa gave signs that such succession would be auspicious, if not his son Huascar was to succeed.

Orders were given to proceed with the ceremony of the calpa, and Cusi Tupac Yupanqui, named by the Inca to be chief steward of the Sun, came to perform it. By the first calpa it was found that the succession of Ninan Cuyoche would not be auspicious. Then they opened another lamb and took out the lungs, examining certain veins. The result was that the signs respecting Huascar were also inauspicious. Returning to the Inca, that he might name some one else, they found that he was dead. While the orejones stood in suspense about the succession, Cusi Tupac Yupanqui said: "Take care of the body, for I go to Tumipampa to give the fringe to Ninan Cuyoche." But when he arrived at Tumipampa he found that Ninan Cuyoche was also dead of the small-pox pestilence[119].

[Note 119: Ninan Cuyoche is said by Cobos to have been legitimate, a son of the first wife Cusi Rimay Huaco, who is said by Sarmiento and others not to have borne a male heir.]

Seeing this Cusi Tupac Yupanqui said to Araua Ocllo—"Be not sad, O Coya! go quickly to Cuzco, and say to your son Huascar that his father named him to be Inca when his own days were over." He appointed two orejones to accompany her, with orders to say to the Incas of Cuzco that they were to give the fringe to Huascar. Cusi Tupac added that he would make necessary arrangements and would presently follow them with the body of Huayna Ccapac, to enter Cuzco with it in triumph, the order of which had been ordained by the Inca on the point of death, on a staff.

Huayna Ccapac died at Quito at the age of 80 years. He left more than 50 sons. He succeeded at the age of 20, and reigned 60 years. He was valiant though cruel.

He left a lineage or ayllu called Tumipampa Ayllu. At present the heads of it, now living, are Don Diego Viracocha Inca, Don Garcia Inguil Tupac, and Gonzalo Sayri. To this ayllu are joined the sons of Paulu Tupac, son of Huayna Ccapac. They are Hanan-cuzcos.

Huayna Ccapac died in the year 1524 of the nativity of our Lord Jesus Christ, the invincible Emperor Charles V of glorious memory being King of Spain, father of your Majesty, and the Pope was Paul III.

The body of Huayna Ccapac was found by the Licentiate Polo in a house where it was kept concealed, in the city of Cuzco. It was guarded by two of his servants named Hualpa Titu and Sumac Yupanqui. His idol or guauqui was called Huaraqui Inca. It was a great image of gold, which has not been found up to the present time.

LXIII. THE LIFE OF HUASCAR, THE LAST INCA, AND OF ATAHUALPA.

Huayna Ccapac being dead, and the news having reached Cuzco, they raised Titu Cusi Hualpa Inti Illapa, called Huascar, to be Inca. He was called Huascar because he was born in a town called Huascar-quihuar, four and a half leagues from Cuzco. Those who remained at Tumipampa embalmed the body of Huayna Ccapac, and collected the spoils and captives taken in his wars, for a triumphal entry into the capital.

It is to be noted that Atahualpa, bastard son of Huayna Ccapac by Tocto Coca, his cousin, of the lineage of Inca Yupanqui, had been taken to that war by his father to prove him. He first went against the Pastos, and came back a fugitive, for which his father rated him severely. Owing to this Atahualpa did not appear among the troops, and he spoke to the Inca orejones of Cuzco in this manner. "My Lords! you know that I am a son of Huayna Ccapac and that my father took me with him, to prove me in the war. Owing to the disaster with the Pastos, my father insulted me in such a way that I could not appear among the troops, still less at Cuzco among my relations who thought that my father would leave me well, but I am left poor and dishonoured. For this reason I have determined to remain here where my father died, and not to live among those who will be pleased to see me poor and out of favour. This being so you need not wait for me." He then embraced them all and took leave of them. They departed with tears and grief, leaving Atahualpa at Tumipampa[120].

[Note 120: Atahualpa is said by Sarmiento and Yamqui Pachacuti to have been an illegitimate son of Huayna Ccapac by Tocto Coca his cousin, of the ayllu of Pachacuti. Cieza de Leon says that he was a son by a woman of Quilaco named Tupac Palla. Gomara, who is followed by Velasco, says that Atahualpa was the son of a princess of Quito. As Huayna Ccapac only set out for the Quito campaign twelve years before his death, and Atahualpa was then grown up, his mother cannot have been a woman of Quito. I, therefore, have no doubt that Sarmiento is right.]

The orejones brought the body of Huayna Ccapac to Cuzco, entering with great triumph, and his obsequies were performed like those of his ancestors. This being done, Huascar presented gold and other presents, as well as wives who had been kept closely confined in the house of the acllas during the time of his father. Huascar built edifices where he was born, and in Cuzco he erected the houses of Amaru-cancha, where is now the monastery of the "Name of Jesus," and others on the Colcampata, where Don Carlos lives, the son of Paulo.

After that he summoned Cusi Tupac Yupanqui, and the other principal orejones who had come with the body of his father, and who were of the lineage of Inca Yupanqui and therefore relations of the mother of Atahualpa. He asked them why they had not brought Atahualpa with them, saying that doubtless they had left him there, that he might rebel at Quito, and that when he did so, they would kill their Inca at Cuzco. The orejones, who had been warned of this suspicion, answered that they knew nothing except that Atahualpa remained at Quito, as he had stated publicly, that he might not be poor and despised among his relations in Cuzco. Huascar, not believing what they said, put them to the torture, but he extracted nothing further from them. Huascar considered the harm that these orejones had done, and that he never could be good friends with them or be able to trust them, so he caused them to be put to death. This gave rise to great lamentation in Cuzco and hatred of Huascar among the Hanan-cuzcos, to which party the deceased belonged. Seeing this Huascar publicly said that he divorced and separated himself from relationship with the lineages of the Hanan-cuzcos because they were for Atahualpa who was a traitor, not having come to Cuzco to do homage. Then he declared war with Atahualpa and assembled troops to send against him. Meanwhile Atahualpa sent his messengers to Huascar with presents, saying that he was his vassal, and as such he desired to know how he could serve the Inca. Huascar rejected the messages and presents of Atahualpa and they even say that he killed the messengers. Others say that he cut their noses and their clothing down to their waists, and sent them back insulted.

While this was taking place at Cuzco the Huancavilcas rebelled. Atahualpa assembled a great army, nominating as captains—Chalco Chima, Quiz-quiz, Incura Hualpa, Rumi-ñaui, Yupanqui, Urco-huaranca and Uña Chullo. They marched against the Huancavilcas, conquered them, and inflicted severe punishment. Returning to Quito, Atahualpa sent a report to Huascar of what had taken place. At this time Atahualpa received news of what Huascar had done to his messengers, and of the death of the orejones; also that Huascar was preparing to make war on him, that he had separated himself from the Hanan-cuzcos, and that he had proclaimed him, Atahualpa, a traitor, which they call aucca. Atahualpa, seeing the evil designs entertained by his brother against him, and that he must prepare to defend himself, took counsel with his captains. They were of one accord that he should not take the field until he had assembled more men, and collected as large an army as possible, because negotiations should be commenced when he was ready for battle.

At this time an Orejon named Hancu and another named Atoc came to Tumipampa to offer sacrifices before the image of Huayna Ccapac, by order of Huascar. They took the wives of Huayna Ccapac and the insignia of Inca without communication with Atahualpa. For this Atahualpa seized them and, being put to the torture, they confessed what orders Huascar had given them, and that an army was being sent against Atahualpa. They were ordered to be killed, and drums to be made of their skins. Then Atahualpa sent scouts along the road to Cuzco, to see what forces were being sent against him by his brother. The scouts came in sight of the army of Huascar and brought back the news.

Atahualpa then marched out of Quito to meet his enemies. The two armies encountered each other at Riopampa where they fought a stubborn and bloody battle, but Atahualpa was victorious. The dead were so numerous that he ordered a heap to be made of their bones, as a memorial. Even now, at this day, the plain may be seen, covered with the bones of those who were slain in that battle.

At this time Huascar had sent troops to conquer the nations of Pumacocha, to the east of the Pacamoros, led by Tampu Usca Mayta and by Titu Atauchi, the brother of Huascar. When the news came of this defeat at Riopampa, Huascar got together another larger army, and named as captains Atoc, Huaychac, Hanco, and Huanca Auqui. This Huanca Auqui had been unfortunate and lost many men in his campaign with the Pacamoros. His brother, the Inca Huascar, to insult him, sent him gifts suited to a woman, ridiculing him. This made Huanca Auqui determine to do something worthy of a man. He marched to Tumipampa, where the army of Atahualpa was encamped to rest after the battle. Finding it without watchfulness, he attacked and surprised the enemy, committing much slaughter.

Atahualpa received the news at Quito, and was much grieved that his brother Huanca Auqui should have made this attack, for at other times when he could have hit him, he had let him go, because he was his brother. He now gave orders to Quiz-quiz and Chalco Chima to advance in pursuit of Huanca Auqui. They overtook him at Cusi-pampa, where they fought and Huanca Auqui was defeated, with great loss on both sides. Huanca Auqui fled, those of Atahualpa following in pursuit as far as Caxamarca, where Huanca Auqui met a large reinforcement sent by Huascar in support. Huanca Auqui ordered them to march against Chalco Chima and Quiz-quiz while he remained at Caxamarca. The troops sent by Huanca Auqui were Chachapoyas and many others, the whole numbering 10,000. They met the enemy and fought near Caxamarca. But the Chachapoyas were defeated and no more than 3000 escaped. Huanca Auqui then fled towards Cuzco, followed by the army of Atahualpa.

In the province of Bombon[121], Huanca Auqui found a good army composed of all nations, which Huascar had sent to await his enemies there, who were coming in pursuit. Those of Atahualpa arrived and a battle was fought for two days without either party gaining an advantage. But on the third day Huanca Auqui was vanquished by Quiz-quiz and Chalco Chima. [Note 121: Correctly Pumpu.]

Huanca Auqui escaped from the rout and came to Xauxa, where he found a further reinforcement of many Indians, Soras, Chancas, Ayamarcas, and Yanyos, sent by his brother. With these he left Xauxa and encountered the pursuing enemy at a place called Yanamarca. Here a battle was fought not less stubbornly than the former one. Finally, as fortune was against Huanca Auqui, he was again defeated by Chalco Chima, the adventurous captain of the army of Atahualpa.

The greater part of the forces of Huanca Auqui was killed. He himself fled, never stopping until he reached Paucaray. Here he found a good company of orejones of Cuzco, under a captain named Mayta Yupanqui who, on the part of Huascar, rebuked Huanca Auqui, asking how it was possible for him to have lost so many battles and so many men, unless he was secretly in concert with Chalco Chima. He answered that the accusation was not true, that he could not have done more; and he told Mayta Yupanqui to go against their enemy, and see what power he brought. He said that Atahualpa was determined to advance if they could not hinder his captains. Then Mayta Yupanqui went on to encounter Chalco Chima, and met him at the bridge of Anco-yacu where there were many skirmishes, but finally the orejones were defeated[122].

[Note 122: This campaign is also fully described by Balboa, and in some detail by Yamqui Pachacuti, pp. 113—116.]

LXIV. HUASCAR INCA MARCHES IN PERSON TO FIGHT CHALCO CHIMA AND QUIZ-QUIZ, THE CAPTAINS OF ATAHUALPA.

As the fortune of Huascar and his captains, especially of Huanca Auqui, was so inferior to that of Atahualpa and his adventurous and dexterous captains Chalco Chima and Quiz-quiz, one side meeting with nothing that did not favour them, the other side with nothing that was not against them, such terrible fear took possession of Huanca Auqui and the other Inca captains after the battle of Anco-yacu bridge, that they fled without stopping to Vilcas, 20 and more leagues from Anco-yacu, on the road to Cuzco.

Over the satisfaction that the captains of Atahualpa felt at the glory of so many victories that they had won, there came the news sent by Atahualpa that he had come in person to Caxamarca and Huamachuco, that he had been received as Inca by all the nations he had passed, and that he had assumed the fringe and the Ccapac-uncu. He was now called Inca of all the land, and it was declared that there was no other Inca but him. He ordered his captains to march onwards conquering, until they encountered Huascar. They were to give him battle, conquer him like the rest, and if possible take him prisoner. Atahualpa was so elated by his victories, and assumed such majesty, that he did not cease to talk of his successes, and no one dared to raise his eyes before him. For those who had business with him he appointed a lieutenant called "Inca Apu," which means "the Inca's lord," who was to take his place by the Inca when he was seated. Those who had business transacted it with him, entering with a load on their backs, and their eyes on the ground, and thus they spoke of their business with the Apu. He then reported to Atahualpa, who decided what was to be done. Atahualpa was very cruel, he killed right and left, destroyed, burnt, and desolated whatever opposed him. From Quito to Huamachuco he perpetrated the greatest cruelties, robberies, outrages, and tyrannies that had ever been done in that land.

When Atahualpa arrived at Huamachuco, two principal lords of his house came to offer sacrifice to the huaca of Huamachuco for the success that had attended their cause. These orejones went, made the sacrifice, and consulted the oracle. They received an answer that Atahualpa would have an unfortunate end, because he was such a cruel tyrant and shedder of so much human blood. They delivered this reply of the devil to Atahualpa. It enraged him against the oracle, so he called out his guards and went to where the huaca was kept. Having surrounded the place, he took a halberd of gold in his hand, and was accompanied by the two officers of his household who had made the sacrifice. When he came to where the idol was, an old man aged a hundred years came out, clothed in a dress reaching down to the ground, very woolly and covered with sea shells. He was the priest of the oracle who had made the reply. When Atahualpa knew who he was, he raised the halberd and gave him a blow which cut off his head. Atahualpa then entered the house of the idol, and cut off its head also with many blows, though it was made of stone. He then ordered the old man's body, the idol, and its house to be burnt, and the cinders to be scattered in the air. He then levelled the hill, though it was very large, where that oracle, idol or huaca of the devil stood.

All this being made known to Chalco Chima and Quiz-quiz, they celebrated festivals and rejoicings, and then resumed their march towards Cuzco. Huascar received reports of all that had happened, and mourned over the great number of men he had lost. He clearly saw that there only remained the remedy of going forth in person to try his fortune, which had hitherto been so adverse. In preparation he kept some fasts—for these gentiles also have a certain kind of fasting, made many sacrifices to the idols and oracles of Cuzco, and sought for replies. All answered that the event would be adverse to him. On hearing this he consulted his diviners and wizards, called by them umu, who, to please him, gave him hope of a fortunate ending. He got together a powerful army, and sent out scouts to discover the position of the enemy. The hostile army was reported to be at a place, 14 leagues from Cuzco, called Curahuasi[123]. They found there Chalco Chima and Quiz-quiz, and reported that they had left the main road to Cuzco, and had taken that of Cotabamba, which is on the right, coming from Caxamarca or Lima to Cuzco. This route was taken to avoid the bad road and dangerous pass by the Apurimac bridge.

Huascar divided his army into three divisions. One consisted of the men of Cunti-suyu, Charcas, Colla-suyu, Chuys, and Chile under the command of a captain named Arampa Yupanqui. His orders were to advance over Cotabamba towards another neighbouring province of the Omasayos, to harass the enemy on the side of the river of Cotabamba and the Apurimac bridge. The survivors of the former battles, under Huanca Auqui, Ahua Panti, and Pacta Mayta, were to attack the enemy on one flank, and to march into Cotabamba. Huascar in person commanded a third division. Thus all the forces of both Huascar and Atahualpa were in Cotabamba.

[Note 123: Curahuasi is near the bridge over the Apurimac.]

Arampa Yupanqui got news that the forces of Atahualpa were passing through a small valley or ravine which leads from Huanacu-pampa. He marched to oppose them, and fought with a strong squadron of the troops under Chalco Chima. He advanced resolutely to the encounter, and slew many of the enemy, including one of their captains named Tomay Rima. This gave Huascar great satisfaction and he said laughingly to the orejones—"The Collas have won this victory. Behold the obligation we have to imitate our ancestors." Presently the captains-general of his army, who were Titu Atauchi, Tupac Atao his brother, Nano, Urco Huaranca and others, marshalled the army to fight those of Atahualpa with their whole force. The armies confronted each other and attacked with skill and in good order.

The battle lasted from morning nearly until sunset, many being slain on both sides, though the troops of Huascar did not suffer so much as those of Chalco Chima and Quiz-quiz. The latter seeing their danger, many of them retreated to a large grassy plateau which was near, in Huanacu-pampa. Huascar, who saw this, set fire to the grass and burnt a great part of Atahualpa's forces.

Chalco Chima and Quiz-quiz then retreated to the other side of the river Cotabamba. Huascar, satisfied with what he had done, did not follow up his advantages, but enjoyed the victory which fortune had placed in his hands. For this he took a higher position. Chalco Chima and Quiz-quiz, who were experienced in such manoeuvres, seeing that they were not followed, decided to rest their troops, and on another day to attack those who believed themselves to be conquerors. They sent spies to the camp of Huascar, and found from them that Huascar would send a certain division of his troops to take Atahualpa's captains, without their being able to escape.

LXV. THE BATTLE BETWEEN THE ARMIES OF HUASCAR AND ATAHUALPA HUASCAR MADE PRISONER.

When the morning of the next day arrived Huascar determined to finish off the army of his brother at one blow. He ordered Tupac Atao to go down the ravine with a squadron, discover the position of the enemy, and report what he had seen. Tupac Atao received this order and entered the ravine in great silence, looking from side to side. But the spies of Chalco Chima saw everything without being seen themselves and gave notice to Chalco Chima and Quiz-quiz. Chalco Chima then divided his men into two parts and stationed them at the sides of the road where the orejones would pass. When Tupac Atao came onwards, they attacked him to such purpose that scarcely any one escaped, Tupac Atao himself was taken, badly wounded, by whom Chalco Chima was informed that Huascar would follow him with only a squadron of 5000 men, while the rest of his army remained in Huanacu-pampa.

Chalco Chima sent this information to Quiz-quiz, who was at a little distance, that they might unite forces. He told him that Tupac Atao was taken, that Huascar was expected with a small force, and that Quiz-quiz was wanted that both might take this enemy on the flanks. This was done. They divided their forces, placing them on both sides as in the attack on Tupac Atao. A short time after they entered the ravine, Huascar and his men came upon the dead bodies of the men of Tupac Atao who, being known to Huascar he wished to turn back, understanding that they were all dead and that there must have been some ambush. But it was too late, for he was surrounded by his enemies. Then he was attacked by the troops of Chalco Chima. When he tried to fly from those who fell upon his rear, he fell into the hands of Quiz-quiz who was waiting for him lower down. Those of Chalco Chima and those of Quiz-quiz fought with great ferocity, sparing none, and killing them all. Chalco Chima, searching for Huascar, saw him in his litter and seized him by the hands, and pulled him out of his litter. Thus was taken prisoner the unfortunate Huascar Inca, twelfth and last tyrant of the Inca Sovereigns of Peru, falling into the power of another greater and more cruel tyrant than himself, his people defeated, killed, and scattered.

Placing Huascar in safe durance with a sufficient guard, Chalco Chima went on in the Inca's litter and detached 5000 of his men to advance towards the other troops remaining on the plain of Huanacu-pampa. He ordered that all the rest should follow Quiz-quiz, and that when he let fall the screen, they should attack. He executed this stratagem because his enemies thought that he was Huascar returning victorious, so they waited. He advanced and arrived where the troops of Huascar were waiting for their lord, who, when they saw him, still thought that it was Huascar bringing his enemies as prisoners. When Chalco Chima was quite near, he let loose a prisoner who had been wounded, who went to the Inca troops. He told them what had happened, that it was Chalco Chima, and that he could kill them all by this stratagem. When this was known, and that Chalco Chima would presently order them to be attacked with his whole force, for he had let the screen fall, which was to be the sign, the Inca troops gave way and took to flight, which was what Chalco Chima intended. The troops of Atahualpa pursued, wounding and killing with excessive cruelty and ferocity, continuing the slaughter, with unheard of havock, as far as the bridge of Cotabamba. As the bridge was narrow and all could not cross it, many jumped into the water from fear of their ferocious pursuers, and were drowned. The troops of Atahualpa crossed the river, continuing the pursuit and rejoicing in their victory. During the pursuit they captured Titu Atauchi, the brother of Huascar. Chalco Chima and Quiz-quiz arrived at some houses called Quiuipay, about half a league from Cuzco, where they placed Huascar as a prisoner with a sufficient guard. Here they encamped and established their head-quarters.

The soldiers of Chalco Chima went to get a view of Cuzco from the hill of Yauina overlooking the city, where they heard the mourning and lamentation of the inhabitants, and returned to inform Chalco Chima and Quiz-quiz. Those captains sent a messenger to Cuzco to tell the inhabitants not to mourn, for that there was nothing to fear, it being well known that this was a war between two brothers for the gratification of their own passions. If any of them had helped Huascar they had not committed a crime, for they were bound to serve their Inca; and if there was any fault he would remit and pardon it, in the name of the great Lord Atahualpa. Presently he would order them all to come out and do reverence to the statue of Atahualpa, called Ticci Ccapac which means "Lord of the World."

The people of Cuzco consulted together, and resolved to come forth and obey the commands of Chalco Chima and Quiz-quiz. They came according to their ayllus and, on arriving at Quiuipay, they seated themselves in that order. Presently the troops of Atahualpa, fully armed, surrounded all those who had come from Cuzco. They took Huanca Auqui, Ahua Panti, and Paucar Usna, who had led the army against them in the battle at Tumipampa. Then they took Apu Chalco Yupanqui and Rupaca, Priests of the Sun, because these had given the fringe to Huascar. These being prisoners Quiz-quiz rose and said—"Now you know of the battles you have fought with me on the road, and the trouble you have caused me. You always raised Huascar to be Inca, who was not the heir. You treated evilly the Inca Atahualpa whom the Sun guards, and for these things you deserve death. But using you with humanity, I pardon you in the name of my Lord Atahualpa, whom may the Sun prosper."

But that they might not be without any punishment, he ordered them to be given some blows with a great stone on the shoulders, and he killed the most culpable. Then he ordered that all should be tied by the knees, with their faces towards Caxamarca or Huamachuco where Atahualpa was, and he made them pull out their eyelashes and eyebrows as an offering to the new Inca. All the orejones, inhabitants of Cuzco, did this from fear, saying in a loud voice, "Long live! Live for many years Atahualpa our Inca, may our father the Sun increase his life!" Araua Ocllo, the mother of Huascar, and his wife Chucuy Huypa, were there, and were dishonoured and abused by Quiz-quiz. In a loud voice the mother of Huascar said to her son, who was a prisoner, "O unfortunate! thy cruelties and evil deeds have brought you to this state. Did I not tell you not to be so cruel, and not to kill nor ill-treat the messengers of your brother Atahualpa." Having said these words she came to him, and gave him a blow in the face. Chalco Chima and Quiz-quiz then sent a messenger to Atahualpa, letting him know all that had happened, and that they had made prisoners of Huascar and many others, and asking for further orders.

LXVI.WHAT CHALCO CHIMA AND QUIZ-QUIZ DID CONCERNING HUASCAR AND THOSE OF HIS SIDE IN WORDS.

After Chalco Chima and Quiz-quiz had sent off the messengers to Atahualpa, they caused the prisoners to be brought before them, and in the presence of all, and of the mother and wife of Huascar, they declared, addressing themselves to the mother of Huascar, that she was the concubine and not the wife of Huayna Ccapac, and that, being his concubine, she had borne Huascar, also that she was a vile woman and not a Coya. The troops of Atahualpa raised a shout of derision, and some said to the orejones, pointing their fingers at Huascar—"Look there at your lord! who said that in the battle he would turn fire and water against his enemies?" Huascar was then tied hand and foot on a bed of ropes of straws. The orejones, from shame, lowered their heads. Presently Quiz-quiz asked Huascar, "Who of these made you lord, there being others better and more valiant than you, who might have been chosen?" Araua Ocllo, speaking to her son, said, "You deserve all this my son as I told you, and all comes from the cruelty with which you treated your own relations." Huascar replied, "Mother! there is now no remedy, leave us," and he addressed himself to the priest Chalco Yupanqui, saying—"Speak and answer the question asked by Quiz-quiz." The priest said to Quiz-quiz, "I raised him to be lord and Inca by command of his father Huayna Ccapac, and because he was son of a Coya" (which is what we should call Infanta). Then Chalco Chima was indignant, and called the priest a deceiver and a liar. Huascar answered to Quiz-quiz, "Leave off these arguments. This is a question between me and my brother, and not between the parties of Hanan-cuzco and Hurin-cuzco. We will investigate it, and you have no business to meddle between us on this point."

Enraged at the answer Chalco Chima ordered Huascar to be taken back to prison, and said to the

Incas, to re-assure them, that they could now go back to the city as they were pardoned. The orejones returned, invoking Viracocha in loud voices with these words—"O Creator! thou who givest life and favour to the Incas where art thou now? Why dost thou allow such persecution to come upon us? Wherefore didst thou exalt us, if we are to come to such an end?" Saying these words they beat their cloaks in token of the curse that had come upon them all.

LXVII.THE CRUELTIES THAT ATAHUALPA ORDERED TO BE PERPETRATED ON THE PRISONERS AND CONQUERED OF HUASCAR'S PARTY.

When Atahualpa knew what had happened, from the messengers of Chalco Chima and Quiz-quiz, he ordered one of his relations named Cusi Yupanqui to go to Cuzco, and not to leave a relation or friend of Huascar alive. This Cusi Yupanqui arrived at Cuzco, and Chalco Chima and Quiz-quiz delivered the prisoners to him. He made inquiries touching all that Atahualpa had ordered. He then caused poles to be fixed on both sides of the road, extending not more than a quarter of a league along the way to Xaquixahuana. Next he brought out of the prison all the wives of Huascar, including those pregnant or lately delivered. He ordered them to be hung to these poles with their children, and he ordered the pregnant to be cut open, and the stillborn to be hung with them. Then he caused the sons of Huascar to be brought out and hung to the poles. Among the sons of Huayna Ccapac who were prisoners there was one named Paullu Tupac. When they were going to kill him, he protested saying, it was unreasonable that he should be killed, because he had previously been imprisoned by Huascar; and on this ground he was released and escaped death. Yet the reason that he was imprisoned by Huascar was because he had been found with one of the Inca's wives. He was only given very little to eat, the intention being that he should die in prison. The woman with whom he was taken was buried alive. The wars coming on he escaped, and what has been related took place.

After this the lords and ladies of Cuzco who were found to have been friends of Huascar were seized and hanged on the poles. Then there was an examination of all the houses of deceased Incas, to see which had been on the side of Huascar, and against Atahualpa. They found that the house of Tupac Inca Yupanqui had sided with Huascar. Cusi Yupanqui committed the punishment of the house to Chalco Chima and Quiz-quiz. They seized the steward of the house, and the mummy of Tupac Inca, and those of his family and hung them all, and they burnt the body of Tupac Inca outside the town and reduced it to ashes. And to destroy the house completely, they killed many mama cunas and servants, so that none were left of that house except a few of no account. Besides this they ordered all the Chachapoyas and Cañaris to be killed, and their Curaca named Ulco Colla, who they said had rebelled against the two brothers. All these murders and cruelties were perpetrated in the presence of Huascar to torment him. They murdered over 80 sons and daughters of Huascar, and what he felt most cruelly was the murder, before his eyes, of one of his sisters named Coya Miro, who had a son of Huascar in her arms, and another in her womb; and another very beautiful sister named Chimbo Cisa. Breaking his heart at the sight of such cruelty and grief which he was powerless to prevent, he cried, with a sigh, "Oh Pachayachachi Viracocha, thou who showed favour to me for so short a time, and honoured me and gave me life, dost thou see that I am treated in this way, and seest thou in thy presence what I, in mine, have seen and see."

Some of the concubines of Huascar escaped from this cruelty and calamity, because they had neither borne a child nor were pregnant, and because they were beautiful. They say that they were kept to be taken to Atahualpa. Among those who escaped were Doña Elvira Chonay, daughter of Cañar Ccapac, Doña Beatriz Carnamaruay, daughter of the Curaca of Chinchay-cocha, Doña Juana Tocto, Doña Catalina Usica, wife, that was, of Don Paullu Tupac, and mother of Don Carlos, who are living now. In this way the line and lineage of the unfortunate tyrant Huascar, the last of the Incas, was completely annihilated.

LXVIII.NEWS OF THE SPANIARDS COMES TO ATAHUALPA.

Atahualpa was at Huamachuco celebrating great festivals for his victories, and he wished to proceed to Cuzco and assume the fringe in the House of the Sun, where all former Incas had received it When he was about to set out there came to him two Tallanas Indians, sent by the Curacas of Payta and Tumbez, to report to him that there had arrived by sea, which they call cocha, a people with different clothing, and with beards, and that they brought animals like large sheep. The chief of them was believed to be Viracocha, which means the god of these people, and he brought with him many Viracochas, which is as much as to say "gods." They said this of the Governor Don Francisco Pizarro, who had arrived with 180 men and some horses which they called sheep. As the account in detail is left for the history of the Spaniards, which will form the Third Part to come after this, I will only here speak briefly of what passed between the Spaniards and Atahualpa.

When this became known to Atahualpa he rejoiced greatly, believing it to be the Viracocha coming, as he had promised when he departed, and as is recounted in the beginning of this history. Atahualpa gave thanks that he should have come in his time, and he sent back the messengers with thanks to the Curacas for sending the news, and ordering them to keep him informed of what might happen. He resolved not to go to Cuzco until he had seen what this arrival was, and what the Viracochas intended to do. He sent orders to Chalco Chima and Quiz-quiz to lose no time in bringing Huascar to Caxamarca, where he would go to await their arrival, for he had received news that certain Viracochas had arrived by sea, and he wished to be there to see what they were like.

As no further news came, because the Spaniards were forming a station at Tangarara, Atahualpa became careless and believed that they had gone. For, at another time, when he was marching with his father, in the wars of Quito, news came to Huayna Ccapac that the Viracocha had arrived on the coast near Tumbez, and then they had gone away. This was when Don Francisco Pizarro came on the first discovery, and returned to Spain for a concession, as will be explained in its place.

LXIX.THE SPANIARDS COME TO CAXAMARCA AND SEIZE ATAHUALPA, WHO ORDERS HUASCAR TO BE KILLED. ATAHUALPA ALSO DIES.

As the subject of which this chapter treats belongs to the Third Part (the history of the Spaniards), I shall here only give a summary of what happened to Atahualpa. Although Atahualpa was careless about the Spaniards they did not miss a point, and when they heard where Atahualpa was, they left Tangarara and arrived at Caxamarca. When Atahualpa knew that the Viracochas were near, he left Caxamarca and went to some baths at a distance of half a league that he might, from there, take the course which seemed best. As he found that they were not gods as he had been made to think at first, he prepared his warriors to resist the Spaniards. Finally he was taken prisoner by Don Francisco Pizarro, the Friar, Vicente Valverde, having first made a certain demand, in the square of Caxamarca.

Don Francisco Pizarro knew of the disputes there had been between Atahualpa and Huascar, and that Huascar was a prisoner in the hands of the captains of Atahualpa, and he urged Atahualpa to have his brother brought as quickly as possible. Huascar was being brought to Caxamarca by Atahualpa's order, as has already been said. Chalco Chima obeying this order, set out with Huascar and the captains and relations who had escaped the butchery of Cusi Yupanqui.

Atahualpa asked Don Francisco Pizarro why he wanted to see his brother. Pizarro replied that he had been informed that Huascar was the elder and principal Lord of that land and for that reason he wished to see him, and he desired that he should come. Atahualpa feared that if Huascar came alive, the Governor Don Francisco Pizarro would be informed of what had taken place, that Huascar would be made Lord, and that he would lose his state. Being sagacious, he agreed to comply with Pizarro's demand, but sent off a messenger to the captain who was bringing Huascar, with an order to kill him and all the prisoners. The messenger started and found Huascar at Antamarca, near Yana-mayu. He gave his message to the captain of the guard who was bringing Huascar as a prisoner.

Directly the captain heard the order of Atahualpa he complied with it. He killed Huascar, cut the body up, and threw it into the river Yana-mayu. He also killed the rest of the brothers, relations, and captains who were with him as prisoners, in the year 1533. Huascar had lived 40 years. He succeeded his father at the age of 31 and reigned for 9 years. His wife was Chucuy Huypa by whom he had no male child. He left no lineage or ayllu, and of those who are now living, one only, named Don Alonso Titu Atauchi is a nephew of Huascar, son of Titu Atauchi who was murdered with Huascar. He alone sustains the name of the lineage of Huascar called the Huascar Ayllu. In this river of Yana-mayu Atahualpa had fixed his boundary pillars when he first rebelled, saying that from thence to Chile should be for his brother Huascar, and from the Yana-mayu onwards should be his. Thus with the death of Huascar there was an end to all the Incas of Peru and all their line and descent which they held to be legitimate, without leaving man or woman who could have a claim on this country, supposing them to have been natural and legitimate lords of it, in conformity with their own customs and tyrannical laws.

For this murder of Huascar, and for other good and sufficient causes, the Governor Don Francisco Pizarro afterwards put Atahualpa to death. He was a tyrant against the natives of this country and against his brother Huascar. He had lived 36 years. He was not Inca of Peru, but a tyrant. He was prudent, sagacious, and valiant, as I shall relate in the Third Part, being events which belong to the deeds of the Spaniards. It suffices to close this Second Part by completing the history of the deeds of the 12 Inca tyrants who reigned in this kingdom of Peru from Manco Ccapac the first to Huascar the twelfth and last tyrant.

LXX. IT IS NOTEWORTHY HOW THESE INCAS WERE TYRANTS AGAINST THEMSELVES, BESIDES BEING SO AGAINST THE NATIVES OF THE LAND.

It is a thing worthy to be noted [for the fact that besides being a thing certain and evident the general tyranny of these cruel and tyrannical Incas of Peru against the natives of the land, may be easily gathered from history], and any one who reads and considers with attention the order and mode of their procedure will see, that their violent Incaship was established without the will and election of the natives who always rose with arms in their hands on each occasion that offered for rising against their Inca tyrants who oppressed them, to get back their liberty. Each one of the

Incas not only followed the tyranny of his father, but also began afresh the same tyranny by force, with deaths, robberies and rapine. Hence none of them could pretend, in good faith, to give a beginning to time of prescription, nor did any of them hold in peaceful possession, there being always some one to dispute and take up arms against them and their tyranny. Moreover, and this is above all to be noted, to understand the worst aims of these tyrants and their horrid avarice and oppression, they were not satisfied with being evil tyrants to the natives, but also to their own proper sons, brothers and relations, in defiance of their own laws and statutes, they were the worst and most pertinacious tyrants with an unheard-of inhumanity. For it was enacted among themselves and by their customs and laws that the eldest legitimate son should succeed, yet almost always they broke the law, as appears by the Incas who are here referred to.

Before all things Manco Ccapac, the first tyrant, coming from Tampu-tocco, was inhuman in the case of his brother Ayar Cachi, sending him to Tampu-tocco cunningly with orders for Tampu-chacay to kill him out of envy, because he was the bravest, and might for that reason be the most esteemed. When he arrived at the valley of Cuzco he not only tyrannized over the natives, but also over Copalimayta and Columchima who, though they had been received as natives of that valley were his relations, for they were orejones. Then Sinchi Rocca, the second Inca, having an older legitimate son named Manco Sapaca who, according to the law he and his father had made, was entitled to the succession, deprived him and nominated Lloqui Yupanqui the second son for his successor. Likewise Mayta Ccapac, the fourth Inca, named for his successor Ccapac Yupanqui, though he had an older legitimate son named Cunti Mayta, whom he disinherited. Viracocha, the eighth Inca, although he had an older legitimate son named Inca Rocca, did not name him as his successor, nor any of his legitimate sons, but a bastard named Inca Urco. This did not come about, Inca Urco did not enjoy the succession, nor did the eldest legitimate son, for there was a new tyranny. For Inca Yupanqui deprived both the one and the other, besides despoiling his father of his honours and estate. The same Inca Yupanqui, having an elder legitimate son named Amaru Tupac Inca, did not name him, but a young son, Tupac Inca Yupanqui. The same Tupac Inca, being of the same condition as his father, having Huayna Ccapac as the eldest legitimate son, named Ccapac Huari as his successor, although the relations of Huayna Ccapac would not allow it, and rose in his favour. If Ccapac Huari was legitimate, as his relations affirm, the evil deed must be fixed on Huayna Ccapac, who deprived his brother Ccapac Huari, and killed his mother and all his relations, making them infamous as traitors, that is supposing he was legitimate. Huayna Ccapac, though he named Ninan Cuyoche, he was not the eldest, and owing to this the succession remained unsettled, and caused the differences between Huascar and Atahualpa, whence proceeded the greatest and most unnatural tyrannies. Turning their arms against their own entrails, robbing, and with inhuman intestine wars they came to a final end. Thus as they commenced by their own authority, so they destroyed all by their own proper hands.

It may be that Almighty God permits that one shall be the executioner of the other for his evil deeds, that both may give place to his most holy gospel which, by the hands of the Spaniards, and by order of the most happy, catholic, and unconquered Emperor and King of Spain, Charles V of glorious memory, father of your Majesty, was sent to these blind and barbarous gentiles. Yet against the force and power of the Incas on foot and united, it appeared that it would be impossible for human force to do what a few Spaniards did, numbering only 180, who at first entered with the Governor Don Francisco Pizarro.

It is well established that it is a thing false and without reason, and which ought not to be said, that there is now, in these kingdoms, any person of the lineage of the Incas who can pretend to a right of succession to the Incaship of this kingdom of Peru, nor to be natural or legitimate lords. For no one is left who, in conformity with their laws, is able to say that he is the heir, in whole or in part of this land. Only two sons of Huayna Ccapac escaped the cruelty of Atahualpa. They were Paullu Tupac, afterwards called Don Cristóval Paullu, and Manco Inca. They were bastards, which is well known among them. And these, if any honour or estate had belonged to them or their children, your Majesty would have granted more than they had, their brothers retaining their estate and power. For they would merely have been their tributaries and servants. These were the lowest of all, for their lineage was on the side of their mothers which is what these people look at, in a question of birth[124].

[Note 124: These statements about the illegitimacy of Manco and Paullu Inca are made to support the Viceroy's argument and have no foundation in fact. The two princes were legitimate; their mother being a princess of the blood.]

And Manco Inca had been a traitor to your Majesty and was a fugitive in the Andes where he died or was killed. Your Majesty caused his son to be brought out, in peace, from those savage wilds. He was named Don Diego Sayri Tupac. He became a Christian, and provision was made for him, his sons and descendants. Sayri Tupac died as a Christian, and he who is now in the Andes in rebellion, named Titu Cusi Yupanqui, is not a legitimate son of Manco Inca, but a bastard and apostate. They hold that another son is legitimate who is with the same Titu, named Tupac Amaru, but he is incapable and the Indians called him uti. Neither one nor the other are heirs of the land, because their father was not legitimate.

Your Majesty honoured Don Cristóval Paullu with titles and granted him a good repartimiento of Indians, on which he principally lived. Now it is possessed by his son Don Carlos. Paullu left two legitimate sons who are now alive, named Don Carlos and Don Felipe. Besides these he left many illegitimate sons. Thus the known grandsons of Huayna Ccapac, who are now alive and admitted to be so, are those above mentioned. Besides these there are Don Alonso Titu Atauchi, son of Titu Atauchi, and other bastards, but neither one nor the other has any right to be called a natural lord of the land.

For the above reasons it will be right to say to those whose duty it may be to decide, that on such clear evidence is based the most just and legitimate title that your Majesty and your successors have to these parts of the Indies, proved by the actual facts that are here written, more especially as regards these kingdoms of Peru without a point to raise against the said titles by which the crown of Spain holds them. Respecting which your Viceroy of these kingdoms, Don Francisco Toledo, has been a careful and most curious enquirer, as zealous for the clearing of the conscience of your Majesty, and for the salvation of your soul, as he has shown and now shows himself in the general visitation which he is making by order of your Majesty, in his own person, not avoiding the very great labours and dangers which he is suffering in these journeys, so long as they result in so great a service to God and your Majesty.

LXXI.SUMMARY COMPUTATION OF THE PERIOD THAT THE INCAS OF PERU LASTED.

The terrible and inveterate tyranny of the Incas Ccapac of Peru, which had its seat in the city of Cuzco, commenced in the year 565 of our Christian redemption, Justin II being Emperor, Loyva son of Athanagild the Goth being King of Spain, and John III Supreme Pontiff. It ended in 1533, Charles V being the most meritorious Emperor and most Christian King of Spain and its dependencies, patron of the church and right arm of Christendom, assuredly worthy of such a son as your Majesty whom may God our Lord take by the hand as is necessary for the Holy Christian church. Paul III was then Pope. The whole period from Manco Ccapac to the death of Huascar was 968 years.

It is not to be wondered at that these Incas lived for so long a time, for in that age nature was stronger and more robust than in these days. Besides men did not then marry until they were past thirty. They thus reached such an age with force and substance whole and undiminished. For these reasons they lived much longer than is the case now. Besides the country where they lived has a healthy climate and uncorrupted air. The land is cleared, dry, without lakes, morasses, or forests with dense vegetation. These qualities all conduce to health, and therefore to the long life of the inhabitants whom may God our Lord lead into his holy faith, for the salvation of their souls. Amen[125].

    Maxima Tolleti Proregis gloria creuit

    Dum regni tenebras, lucida cura, fugat.

    Ite procul scioli, vobis non locus in istis!

    Rex Indos noster nam tenet innocue.

[Note 125: Cieza de Leon and other authorities adopt a more moderate chronology.]

CERTIFICATE OF THE PROOFS AND VERIFICATION OF THIS HISTORY.

In the city of Cuzco, on the 29th day of February, 1572, before the very excellent Lord Don Francisco de Toledo, Mayor-domo to His Majesty, and his Viceroy, Governor, and Captain-General of these kingdoms and provinces of Peru, President of the Royal Audience and Chancellory that resides in the city of the Kings, and before me Alvaro Ruiz de Navamuel his Secretary and of the Government and General Visitation of these kingdoms, the Captain Pedro Sarmiento de Gamboa presented a petition of the following tenor:

Most Excellent Lord,

I, the Captain Pedro Sarmiento, Cosmographer-General of these kingdoms of Peru, report that by order of your Excellency I have collected and reduced to a history the general chronicle of the origin and descent of the Incas, of the particular deeds which each one did in his time and in the part he ruled, how each one of them was obeyed, of the tyranny with which, from the time of Tupac Inca Yupanqui, the tenth Inca, they oppressed and subjugated these kingdoms of Peru until by order of the Emperor Charles V of glorious memory, Don Francisco Pizarro came to conquer them. I have drawn up this history from the information and investigations which, by order of your Excellency, were collected and made in the valley of Xauxa, in the city of Guamanga, and in other parts where your Excellency was conducting your visitation, but principally in this city of Cuzco where the Incas had their continual residence, where there is more evidence of their acts, where the mitimaes of all the provinces gathered together by order of the said Incas, and where there is true memory of their ayllus. In order that this history may have more authority, I pray that you will see, correct, and give it your authority, so that, wherever it may be seen, it may have entire faith and credit.

Pedro Sarmiento de Gamboa.

Having been seen by his Excellency he said that it may be known if the said history was in conformity with the information and evidence, which has been taken from the Indians and other persons of this city and in other parts, and he ordered that Doctor Loarte, Alcalde of the court of his Majesty should cause to appear before him the principal and most intelligent Indians of the twelve ayllus or lineages of the twelve Incas and other persons who may be summoned, and being assembled before me, the present Secretary, the said history shall be read and declared to them by an interpreter in the language of the said Indians, that each one may understand and discuss it among themselves, whether it is conformable to the truth as they know it. If there is anything to correct or amend, or which may appear to be contrary to what they know, it is to be corrected or amended. So I provide and sign

Don Francisco de Toledo

Before me Alvaro Ruiz de Navamuel.

Afterwards, on the abovesaid day, month, and year the illustrious Doctor Gabriel de Loarte, in compliance with the order of his Excellency and in presence of me the said Secretary, caused to appear before him the Indians of the names, ages and ayllus as follows:

Ayllu of Manco Ccapac.

Aged

Sebastian Ylluc 30

Francisco Paucar Chima 30

Ayllu of Sinchi Rocca.

Diego Cayo Hualpa 70

Don Alonso Puzcon 40

Ayllu of Lloqui Yupanqui.

Hernando Hualpa 70

Don Garcia Ancuy 45

Miguel Rimachi Mayta 30

Ayllu of Mayta Ccapac.

Don Juan Tampu Usca Mayta 60

Don Felipe Usca Mayta 70

Francisco Usca Mayta 30

Ayllu of Ccapac Yupanqui.

Aged

Don Francisco Copca Mayta 70

Don Juan Quispi Mayta 30

Don Juan Apu Mayta 30

Ayllu of Inca Rocca. Don Pedro Hachacona 53 Don Diego Mayta 40

Ayllu of Yahuar-huaccac. Juan Yupanqui 60 Martin Rimachi 26

Ayllu of Viracocha.

Don Francisco Anti-hualpa 89

Martin Quichua Sucsu 64

Don Francisco Chalco Yupanqui 45

Ayllu of Pachacuti.

Don Diego Cayo 68

Don Juan Hualpa Yupanqui 75

Don Domingo Pascac 90

Don Juan Quispi Cusi 45

Don Francisco Chanca Rimachi 40

Don Francisco Cota Yupanqui 40

Don Gonzalo Huacanhui 60

Don Francisco Quichua 68

Ayllu of Tupac Inca.

Don Cristóval Pisac Tupac 50

Don Andres Tupac Yupanqui 40
Don Garcia Pilco Tupac 40
Don Juan Cozco 40
    Ayllu of Huayna Ccapac.
Don Francisco Sayri 28
Don Francisco Ninan Coro 24
Don Garcia Rimac Tupac 34
    Ayllu of Huascar.
                    Aged
Don Alonso Titu Atauchi 40
    Besides these Ayllus.
Don Garcia Paucar Sucsu 34
Don Carlos Ayallilla 50
Don Juan Apanca 80
Don Garcia Apu Rinti 70
Don Diego Viracocha Inca 34
Don Gonzalo Tupac 30

These being together in presence of his Excellency, the said Alcalde of the court, by the words of Gonzalo Gomez Ximenes, interpreter to his Excellency, in the general language of the Indians, said:—"His Excellency, desiring to verify and put in writing and to record the origin of the Incas, your ancestors, their descent and their deeds, what each one did in his time, and in what parts each one was obeyed, which of them was the first to go forth from Cuzco to subdue other lands, and how Tupac Inca Yupanqui and afterwards Huayna Ccapac and Huascar, his son and grandson became lords of all Peru by force of arms; and to establish this with more authenticity, he has ordered that information and other proofs should be supplied in this city and other parts, and that the said information and proofs should be, by Captain Pedro Sarmiento to whom they were delivered, digested into a true history and chronicle. The said Pedro Sarmiento has now made it and presented it to his Excellency, to ascertain whether it is truthfully written in conformity with the sayings and declarations which were made by some Indians of the said ayllus. His Excellency is informed that the ayllus and descendants of the twelve Incas have preserved among themselves the memory of the deeds of their ancestors, and are those who best know whether the said chronicle is correct or defective, he has therefore caused you to assemble here, that it may be read in your presence and understood. You, among yourselves, will discuss what will be read and declared in the said language, and see if it agrees with the truth as you know it, and that you may feel a stronger obligation to say what you know, it is ordered that you take an oath."

The said Indians replied that they had understood why they had been sent for, and what it was that was required. They then swore, in the said language, by God our Lord, and by the sign of the cross, that they would tell the truth concerning what they knew of that history. The oaths being taken the reading was commenced in sum and substance. There was read on that and following days from their fable of the creation to the end of the history of the Incas. As it was read, so it was interpreted into their language, chapter by chapter. And over each chapter the Indians discussed and conferred among themselves in the said language. All were agreed in confirming and declaring through the interpreter, that the said history was good and true, and in agreement with what they knew and had heard their fathers and ancestors say, as it had been told to them. For, as they have no writing like the Spaniards, they conserve ancient traditions among themselves by passing them from tongue to tongue, and age to age. They heard their fathers and ancestors say that Pachacuti Inca Yupanqui, the ninth Inca, had verified the history of the former Incas who were before him, and painted their deeds on boards, whence also they had been able to learn the sayings of their fathers, and had passed them on to their children. They only amended some names of persons and places and made other slight corrections, which the said Alcalde ordered to be inserted as the Indians had spoken, and this was done. After the said corrections all the Indians, with one accord, said that the history was good and true, in conformity with what they knew and had heard from their ancestors, for they had conferred and discussed among themselves, verifying from beginning to end. They expressed their belief that no other history that might be written could be so authentic and true as this one, because none could have so diligent an examination, from those who are able to state the truth. The said Alcalde signed

The Doctor Loarte

Gonzalo Gomez Ximenes

Before me Alvaro Ruiz de Navamuel.

After the above, in the said city of Cuzco, on the 2nd of March of the same year, his Excellency having seen the declaration of the Indians and the affidavits that were made on them, said that he ordered and orders that, with the corrections the said Indians stated should be made, the history should be sent to his Majesty, signed and authenticated by me the said Secretary. It was approved and signed by the said Doctor Gabriel de Loarte who was present at the verification with the Indians, and then taken and signed

Don Francisco de Toledo

Before Alvaro Ruiz de Navamuel

I the said Alvaro Ruiz de Navamuel, Secretary to his Excellency, of the Government, and to the general visitation of these kingdoms, notary to his Majesty, certify that the said testimony and verification was taken before me, and is taken from the original which remains in my possession, and that the said Alcalde, the Doctor Loarte, who signed, said that he placed and interposed upon it his authority and judicial decree, that it may be valued and accepted within his jurisdiction and beyond it. I here made my sign in testimony of the truth

Alvaro Ruiz de Navamuel